STORIES FROM THE SIDELINES

STORIES
FROM THE
SIDELINES

BY KEVIN E. HEENAN

XULON PRESS

Xulon Press
2301 Lucien Way #415
Maitland, FL 32751
407.339.4217
www.xulonpress.com

Paperback ISBN-13: 978-1-6628-4670-0
Ebook ISBN-13: 978-1-6628-4671-7

FOREWORD

By Coach Rhett Soliday

W ISDOM. What is it and how is it attained? The older I get the more I see the deep desires of the heart shift in my life. I turned 40 this year, and with a wife, 3 kids, a mortgage, and a career in leadership, I have found that often times the areas where I thought I was so smart and the things that I just "knew" to be true are now being challenged every day. Not only that, but as my pastor once stated, as people we often are faced with two choices: Choosing to be right or choosing to be wise. Another way to say it is what used to matter to me a lot just doesn't matter as much anymore. Being married for 17 years has shown me that there is much more value in being wise than being right.

I love the book of Proverbs in the Bible because it truly is a book of wisdom. One of my favorites is found in Proverbs 3:13-17 and it says: "Blessed are those who find wisdom, those who gain understanding, for she is more profitable than silver and yields better returns than gold. She is more precious than rubies; nothing you desire can compare with her. Long life is in her right hand; in her left hand are riches and honor. Her ways are pleasant ways, and all her paths are peace."

The greatest leaders in history are men and women who pursued wisdom before being right. Lord, make me this kind of leader! One of the best ways to glean wisdom is from those around us whose life experiences and thoughtful reflections on those experiences provide a lighted path for a journey we may soon be on. In my life, Kevin Heenan has been a hero of wisdom to me. As a coach on our staff, nobody would know that amongst all the coaches and players in our program that Kevin was BY FAR the best player among us all. Nobody else on our staff was one of the all-time greats in Orange County California basketball history and he led Cal State Fullerton to an elite 8 in his college days, and oh by the way also got drafted by the Golden State Warriors of the NBA. None of my players know that unless I TELL THEM. Coach Heenan has wisdom. He understands that none of our men will care how much he knows until they know how much he cares. Then, when he speaks, guess what happens? You got it, they ALL listen.

Timeless wisdom like this and so many other words and actions are what I glean from Kevin Heenan every day that I spend with him. He is an amazing husband, father, grandfather, and man of God who has an amazing life story, and he has reflected on that story. His reflections are captured in this book, and I'm so excited for you to glean from a man that I count not only as a friend, but as one of my mentors and heroes.

TABLE OF CONTENTS

INTRODUCTION

T he stories and poems written in this book, *Stories from the Sidelines,* came about from the task I took on as an assistant basketball coach at Vanguard University (VU) to help our players understand that there is more to life than just basketball. Through my writings, I tried to impart words to the team so they might know how hard life can be, how much a blessing life actually is, and to have an understanding that nothing in this life is perfect. However, if we decide to walk out our lives with a personal relationship with God, it can define our lives in wonderful and holy ways and give our lives the meaning that God intended them to have. In these writings from *Stories from the Sidelines,* you'll read about hope, God's infinite power to work in one's life, staying the course, Scripture verses, and the power of prayer. I talk about many topics, and each little story is usually followed up with a poem that I wrote about the story or situation.

My inspirations for stories and poems came from our coaching staff and players that I coached with as they rode the roller-coaster life of being a college basketball player and student. Years ago I lived out my basketball dreams. I started playing basketball in 1965 (age eight) and fell in love with it immediately. Along the way through high school and college, I experienced personal and team successes. After college I was considered good enough to get drafted by the Golden State Warriors; however, I never officially played in the National Basketball Association (NBA). I did play in the Pro Summer League, and I played for Athletes in Action (Campus Crusade for Christ) and also in France for some time. Even though my lifelong dream was to play in the NBA, I consider myself blessed to have had the experiences in basketball that I still carry with me today.

I became a member of the men's basketball staff at VU during the 2012–2013 season. During the 2013–2014 season, our team won the national championship of the National Association of Intercollegiate Athletics (NAIA) men's basketball title. It was quite the accomplishment, for sure, and one I'll never forget. But the seasons always come to an end, much like the seasons in our own lives. In this tournament we won, there were sixty-three other teams that went home unhappy. Yet the sun still rose the next day for us and for them. Life's victories and losses are written about in the following pages. Over my years, I've learned that in the end, this life is simply better when we walk hand in hand with God.

Our head coach, Rhett Soliday, is a master at teaching God's love for all of us, and I'm so delighted and blessed that I actually found a place on his staff. He does the x's and o's of basketball really well, and he does the x's and o's of life even better. Unfortunately, for us we all had to navigate our way through the COVID-19 pandemic and it really interrupted our 2020-2021 campaign. Everybody worldwide had to take steps backwards as we worked through the new issues of the days.

I'm completing my book during our 2021-2022 campaign and it's exciting to be somewhat back to normal but COVID-19 will still rear its ugly head from time to time. Lastly, as a team, Vanguard University will be moving forward in the future by building itself a new arena to play our games in and also having classrooms, athletic training facilities, weight rooms and general lobby areas. Yes, it's certainly been an exciting ten plus years being involved with the Vanguard University men's basketball program. Thank you to all the people I've come in contact over the years and contributing to the themes set forth in the following pages.

THE PIT

The Pit. Home of the Vanguard Lions. Though built in the 1940's, its name was given in the 1970's when opposing coaches gave it that name because they disliked playing events there. Standing now for over eighty years, the bleachers come right to the sideline of play, which creates a highly intense venue for both the players and fans alike. With standing room only, over 900 fans have packed in for home games. The facility has been host to over 1,000 victories for the Blue and Gold including 17 Golden State Athletic Conference Championships and two NAIA National Championships.

I've played basketball all over the world and in some of the nicest arenas with capacities ranging from one thousand to twenty thousand. Some of my favorites have included Pauley Pavilion (UCLA), Jennison Fieldhouse (Michigan State), St. John Arena (Ohio State), Kansas City Municipal Auditorium (where we won NAIA National Championship), Stockton Civic Auditorium (University of the Pacific), Long Beach Arena (Long Beach State), and of course my home court throughout college, Titan Gym, at Cal State Fullerton.

I also played at two other arenas aptly named The Pit. The University of Oregon's basketball team played at McArthur

Court, aka, The Pit, in Eugene, Oregon. Ten thousand maniacs would cram into this place and rock and roll the whole game. It was intimate and entertaining and I have to admit it was hard to block out all the noise.

Another favorite place named The Pit was located at the home of the New Mexico Lobos in Albuquerque, New Mexico. In 1999, Sports Illustrated did a story on the top twenty sports venues of the Century and The Pit was named at number thirteen, behind the likes of Yankee Stadium, Augusta National Golf Course, and Wrigley Field to name a few. Arguably one of the best highlights of my basketball career happened at The Pit in Albuquerque. In the 1977-1978 basketball season, in my junior year in college at Cal State Fullerton, we made the NCAA basketball tournament. We had to play a first round game against New Mexico and that game was played at Arizona State University, with the winner to advance to Western Regional Finals at The Pit in Albuquerque. Basically, New Mexico was playing us on a neutral court and if they won they returned home to The Pit to play their next two games to advance to the Final Four. However, we beat them on this day in Arizona and their season was finished. Needless to say when we came to Albuquerque to play our games we were greeted with much hostility. The boos were deafening and the words spewed at us in warm ups and for the time we were there are memorable to say the least. We did end up losing in the Western Regional Finals by three points to University of Arkansas and falling just short in our bid to make it to The Final Four. But what a memorable five days at this Pit.

With all the arenas I've competed in, I'd have to say The Pit at Vanguard University is at the top of my list. My son Dennis played basketball at The Pit from 2006-2010. My daughters Jamie and Kelly competed in Volleyball from 2008-2014 at The Pit. My daughter in law Kelsey competed in basketball from 2007-2009 and I've been coaching at The Pit since 2012. Those years add up to close to Three Hundred Fifty home games that I've been a part of at The Pit. I've experienced some memorable victories and pain staking losses at The Pit over the years, but The Pit will remain a special place to me always.

In the Spring of 2022 there are plans to tear The Pit down and build a new arena, to be called Freed Center for Leadership and Service. Completion date is scheduled for some time in 2024. It'll be up to date and have all the bells and whistles of modern society. This new venue will undoubtedly bring new memories for years to come.

THE PIT
By Kevin E. Heenan

You've stood the tests of time,
And you wavered but never quit.
Oh the many times we cheered,
At the place they called The Pit.

The victories were so many,
And the crowds they always roared.
Games were won and games were lost,
Upon these cherished hardwood floors.

There were always pre-game prayers,
Before each contest that was played.
Thanks were given for the blessings we had,
Was something that was always prayed.

Sometimes in the quiet of The Pit,
I would wonder if you'd ever be gone.
Would they ever think of saying good bye?
Or forever just leave you alone?

In your waning days this much is true,
It's your time to be put to rest.
You've created such wonderful memories,
And for those memories we're certainly blessed.

So farewell my friend, you've served us well,
That is something we will all admit.
You were special and humble and you will be missed,
At the place they called The Pit.

4

GOD IS GOD

Sometimes in our existence we foolishly struggle when all we really need to remember is that GOD IS GOD! Psalm 77:14 reminds us that "You are the God who performs miracles; You display Your power among the peoples." If GOD IS GOD, let's trust in Him that He has our lives in the palms of His hands. Let's keep learning to let go and let God.

Let's not forget that with God on our side...

- There is no prayer too big for God to answer.
- There is no problem too big for God to solve.
- There is no disease God cannot heal.
- There is no heart God cannot mend.
- There is no relationship God cannot restore.
- There is no person God cannot save.
- There is no chaos to which God cannot bring order.
- There is no anxiety to which God cannot bring peace.

There is no disaster to which God cannot bring joy.

- There is no loss to which God cannot bring hope.
- There is no defeat to which God cannot bring victory.
- There is no death to which God cannot bring life.

- There is no suffering to which God cannot bring relief.
- There is no past God cannot redeem.
- There is no sin God cannot forgive.
- There is no bondage God cannot break.
- There is no need God cannot meet.
- There is no enemy God cannot defeat.

There is no mountain God cannot move.

- There is no promise too big for God to fulfill.
- God has you in the palm of His hands. Read Isaiah 49:16.

God can provide fulfillment to our lives. He can solve our problems and heal us and restore us. He can bring order and peace and save us from life's dilemmas. He can bring us peace and joy and hope. In His forgiveness He can bring us relief in the life that we live, and He can move any mountain. Take us as we are, Lord, and lead us and shape us. Open our eyes as we recognize that it's good to be by Your side... in the palms of Your hands.

HERE WE ARE
By Kevin E. Heenan

Here we are, Lord,
You be in the lead.
Create a path for us,
You're our biggest need.

Here we are, Lord,
Yours to shape and mold.
Form us into Your likeness,
Make us strong and bold.

Here we are, Lord,
Humbly on our knees.
Open our hearts and eyes,
It's You we want to see.

Here we are, Lord,
We need You by our side.
Keep us protected from the enemy,
In You we want to abide.

Here we are, Lord,
We are safe within Your arms.
Protect us from the world's ways,
Shelter us from all life's storms.

Here we are, Lord,
With You we want to stand.
We're thankful that You're here,
As You hold us within Your hands.

HOPE IN TODAY

F AITH makes all things possible, LOVE makes all things easy, and HOPE makes all things work. It got me to thinking how important HOPE is to our successes in life. In all things, it is better to hope than it is to despair, right? So, let's not lose HOPE in today, no matter how difficult it is.

Some mornings we wake up and it's "good morning, God," and other mornings we wake up and it's "good God, it's morning." There are those moments in life where we've lost hope in the situations of what life throws our way. Everybody loses their hope from time to time. We are pushing toward our goals and dreams, but obstacles get in the way, causing us to lose sight of the big picture instead of keeping focused on the hope that we have.

Hope is simply defined as the expectation of good things to come. It is steeped in a deeper belief and a faith that proves that things tend to work in our favor in the long run. It begs the question, how do we avoid losing hope?

A couple of ideas to help us keep our HOPES UP might be as follows:

1. Maybe we need to *reassess* our situation. Maybe this goal we were striving for is something we really don't want or shouldn't have wanted in the first place. Maybe we didn't check all the boxes we should have when starting down what appears to be the wrong path. Our hopes have been cracked a little bit because we've seen no growth in our endeavor. There is no loss in reassessing where we stand, so do it if you feel like you're losing hope.

2. Going hand in hand with reassessing losing hope in a situation is to be honest with yourself. Honesty will always breed awareness of when you're trying to accomplish something. Be honest with yourself, and don't try to be something you're not. Seeking out others' opinions is of utmost importance. You can't possibly live long enough to make all the mistakes in the world. Sometimes the waves of life are choppy indeed, and you need to keep in mind there are others who might have gone through what you're going through. Let them be a voice of reason.

3. And finally, you've got to find some scriptures from God's Word that you can take along beside you to stay in the fight. We've got to have a little faith. By having faith, we can learn to understand that nothing is impossible to overcome. No situation can defeat you if you don't want it to. Having faith comes from within and keeps our HOPES alive.

Here are some scriptures to take along with you to keep your HOPE alive (all emphasis has been added):

ISAIAH 40:31: "But those that HOPE in the Lord will renew their strength. They will soar on wings like eagles; they will run and not grow weary, they will walk and not be faint."

JEREMIAH 29:11: "'For I know the plans I have for you,' declares the Lord, 'plans to prosper you and not to harm you, plans to give you HOPE and a future.'"

PSALM 42:5: "Why, my soul, are you downcast? Why so disturbed within me? Put your HOPE in God, for I will yet praise Him, my Savior and my God."

PSALM 25:3: "No one who HOPES in You will ever be put to shame."

PSALM 33:18: "But the eyes of the Lord are on those who fear Him, on those whose HOPE is in His unfailing love."

PSALM 31:24: "Be strong and take heart, all you who HOPE in the Lord."

When HOPE deferred makes your heart sick, look to Jesus. "But now, Lord, what do I look for? My hope is in You" (Ps. 39:7).

HOPE IN TODAY
By Kevin E. Heenan

Has your heart ever said that it's had enough?
And life is never easy and always rough.
You just want to move on, have it all go away,
But you must continue to hope, hope in today.

The feeling is gone of what is the norm,
And clouds are everywhere, storm after storm.
Blue skies gone and you're speechless without say,
But you must continue to hope, hope in today.

Rock bottom is here with no peaks in sight,
Even the daytimes are embraced by the sleepless night.
Everything seems helpless, like there isn't any way,
But you must continue to hope, hope in today.

Hope is always there for you to hold,
Let God take over so He can shape and mold.
He knows the price you've had to pay,
So you must continue in hope, hope in today.

If it ever looks like you're not going anywhere,
And life's problems are just too hard to bear,
Look to the heavens where God will show the way,
Just continue in hope, hope in today.

STAYING THE COURSE

S taying the course is a phrase used in the context of a war or battle, meaning to pursue a goal or continuing to pursue a goal regardless of any obstacles or criticism.

We've all been knocked off course when we are pursuing our dreams and goals as we move through life. IF and WHEN we are derailed from our path, will we maintain our drive and stay the course? It is a given that once we set sail on our journeys, we will encounter obstacles that can knock us off course.

Never give up. In difficult times, we must believe in our hopes and dreams and be willing to see them through. IF we can never give up, our dreams will have success.

Three of my important things to consider in STAYING THE COURSE are listed below:

STAY POSITIVE — Your mental attitude is always of utmost importance. There are always two ways to look at life: either expecting a great outcome (enjoying the journey and not just the destination), OR expecting the worst (and usually in life you get what you expect). Keeping a positive attitude is paramount to STAYING THE COURSE.

BE PERSISTENT — Being persistent is another key ingredient for STAYING THE COURSE. Think of a gardener who plants a seed then waits for it to sprout and grow. He will continue to water and nourish the seed even though he can't see immediate results. Persistence, along with having patience, is the pathway to arriving at a successful destination. Persistent people know that often the hardest times they come across lead to the greatest moments in their lives. With a persistent outlook, you simply know that the storms make you stronger and that they don't last forever. Pursue the day at hand.

SEEK GOD'S DIRECTION — Sometimes this life simply gets hard. Our plans and our hopes get shattered by one thing or another. There will at times seem like there's no way out. We'll ask God, "Why me?" In bad times, we must remind ourselves that God is there to help us through. HE will help us. We have to SEEK Him. God can be our refuge and strength. Let's turn to Him and use His power to keep us on the right paths.

The following verses help me get back on course during times that are tough:

JAMES 1:5-8 "If any of you lacks wisdom, you should ask God, who gives generously to all without finding fault, and it will be given to you. But when you ask, you must believe and not doubt, because the one who doubts is like a wave of the sea, blown and tossed by the wind. That person should not expect to receive anything from the Lord. Such a person is double-minded and unstable in all they do."

EPHESIANS 5:15-17: "Be very careful, then, how you live—not as unwise but as wise, making the most of every opportunity, because the days are evil. Therefore do not be foolish, but understand what the Lord's will is."

PROVERBS 3:5–6: "Trust in the Lord with all your heart and lean not on your understanding; in all your ways submit to Him, and He will make your paths straight."

STAYING THE COURSE is the only way to go. Sometimes it entails taking the Higher Road, the road that is less traveled. This road will make us stronger; it'll cause us to persevere, and it'll make us the winner that God intends us to be. God wants us to take the Higher Road as we try to stay the course in our lives. With a steady hand and a calm demeanor, let's STAY THE COURSE and overcome!

THE HIGHER ROAD
By Kevin E. Heenan

There is a road less traveled by those who live here,
They don't seek it out because it isn't so near.
It lessens the burdens and it lightens the loads,
It's a place that they call the Higher Road.

It offers perspective, forgiveness, and peace,
It offers those hurting a nice little place.
To rest and to revive and to find peace for the soul,
It's a place that they call the Higher Road.

Climb the mountains that this road winds upon,
And seek the treasures buried within its golden ponds.
As you clear through the obstacles that come your own way,
You can look out from the Higher Road and this
is what it will say:

"Thanks for traveling upon Me, I know it hasn't been smooth,
But you did the right thing and you certainly didn't lose.
Let Me tell you I love you and take your heart to the song,
Because the Higher Road's less traveled,
but it's here you belong."

A STORY FOR EVERYBODY

This is a story about four people named Everybody, Somebody, Anybody, and Nobody. There was an important job to be done, and Everybody was sure that Somebody would do it. Anybody could have done it, but Nobody did it. Somebody got angry about that because it was Everybody's job. Everybody thought Anybody could do it, but Nobody realized that Everybody wouldn't do it. It ended up that Everybody blamed Somebody when Nobody did what Anybody could have.

Have you ever been in a life situation like this simple story where you have seen nothing accomplished? It happens in everyday life from business to team sports. If you have been in a team situation, the last sentence is the most compelling: "EVERYBODY BLAMED SOMEBODY WHEN NOBODY DID WHAT ANYBODY COULD HAVE." Anybody could have done it, and Everybody blamed Somebody when Nobody did it.

This little story is a reminder that we need to be that BODY that stands up to any and all challenges and gets the job done. In a lot of cases, people get crippled by worry, anxiety, and fear as it overwhelms them like a thick shadow of darkness, controlling their every move and decision. It's kind of like having a "paralysis through analysis" or "paralysis through overanalysis" situation, which leads to nothing getting done or achieved.

My thought today revolves around finding ways to stay engaged in this stress-filled world we live in. With all the stuff going on around us, we may find ourselves waking up anxious or worried and going to bed the same way. Because we are all human, we often allow our feelings to dictate most of our actions and, for that matter, our inaction—you know, where NOBODY does anything.

Scripture teaches us that we must hide His Word in our hearts so that we don't sin against Him (Ps. 119:11). IF we can start our day with a devotion or quiet time with God, we're off to a good start, but it's nice to have His Word available to us the rest of the day to remain strong. Feelings will come and go during the day, so it's nice to have God's truths available to call on during the day. Having a repertoire of truth is important to have in our back pocket. When we have God's Word readily available and ready to be read and proclaimed, we will be armed to stand firm in our faith and against the negativity this world creates for us all on its own.

Listed below are some of my favorite scriptures that carry me through the days. Copy these below or make up your own favorites to have available on your person for your review during the day so that you know God is with you and is for you.

"This is the day that the Lord has made; let us rejoice and be glad in it" (Ps. 118:24).

17

"Trust in the Lord with all your heart, and do not lean on your understanding. In all your ways acknowledge Him, and He will make straight your paths" (Prov. 3:5–6).

"The Lord will give strength unto His people; the Lord will bless His people with peace" (Ps. 29:11).

"God is our refuge and strength, a very present help in trouble" (Ps. 46:1).

"I can do all things through Christ who strengthens me" (Phil. 4:13).

"'For I know the plans I have for you,' declares the Lord, 'plans to prosper you and not to harm you, plans to give you hope and a future. Then you will call upon Me and come and pray to Me, and I will listen to you. You will seek Me and find Me when you seek Me with all your heart'" (Jer. 29:11–13).

"But I say unto you which hear, love your enemies, do good to them which hate you, bless them that curse you, and pray for them which despitefully use you" (Luke 6:27–28).

"Do not be anxious about anything, but in everything by prayer and supplication with thanksgiving let your requests be made known to God. And the peace of God, which surpasses all understanding, will guard your hearts and your minds in Christ Jesus" (Phil. 4:6–7).

Let's be somebody and shoot for the moon in what we do today. Even IF we miss, we'll still land amongst the stars. Let's remember and learn from yesterday and not worry about tomorrow so we can be all we're supposed to be today. Amen!

THE POWER OF PRAYER

We all enter into prayer in different mindsets. Sometimes we're confused and stressed. Sometimes we're just thankful. Sometimes we're panicked and sideways. But usually when we've finished asking God for His help, we're relieved. "You will keep him in perfect peace, whose mind is stayed on You" from Isaiah 26:3 is an applicable mindset after prayer.

Prayer to almighty God shows us many reasons why we should pray to God, both in triumphs and defeats. Here are some simple points about prayer:

1. I don't know about you, but it seems to me that when I need something, I turn to prayer. Whether it's regarding my children, my job, or money, I've been told that "God is only a prayer away," so I use that as a reminder to pray. When I do begin to pray, it reminds me that God is my source, my healer, my director, and my helper.

2. Prayer seems to help organize my day better when I do it in the morning. It just seems to start the day off in the right way. It gets me oriented at the start of the day so I'm braced to see God at work.

3. With prayer at the beginning of the day, it's also relevant to point out that prayer at the end of the day is

beneficial too. Whereas prayer at the start of day is for pleas of direction and help, prayers at the end of the day seem to offer the thanks that God likes to hear as He got us through another day.

4. Prayer in the morning and evening and even in between reminds us that God is God and He is the one in control of our lives. IF we really want to improve our relationship with God, praying throughout the day is a great way to do that.

5. As Christians, we fail so often in our day-to-day lives. We are human, after all. But when we pray to God, it makes us feel good. It makes our humanness real, not only to us but to God also. It's been said that prayer is the best option we have to make it through this life. Amen to that!

THE POWER OF PRAYER
By Kevin E. Heenan

There is something you must always believe in,
Something that you know will always be there.
It's something you must never underestimate,
And that is the power of prayer.

If you pray to the Lord to guide your life,
He will be there through all your hope and despair.
Offer Him your requests each day and night,
As you trust in the power of prayer.

The Lord who reigns in the heavens above,
Is always available through life's affairs.
He wants us to find Him in all that we do,
And He wants us to yield to the power of prayer.

Life's little problems and the big ones too,
Will always be present for us to bear.
It's at times like these, we must get on our knees,
And find our solace through the power of prayer.

God always hears us through the words that we pray,
We have a God to whom nothing else compares.
So much can be accomplished in each of our lives,
If we simply believe in the power of prayer.

IN THE END

In mid-March 2019, I was in Kansas City for the NAIA (National Association of Intercollegiate Athletics) men's basketball tournament. As a coach the pinnacle to the basketball year is making the national tournament. So this year was certainly a special year.

Thirty-two teams from across the country gathered in Kansas City with the hopes of staying ten days to play for a championship. Unfortunately, we lost in our first-round game to a good team from William Penn University, Iowa, and just like that, our season was over—no more practices, no more prepping for games, no more games to be played, no more airport travel, and no more camaraderie with teammates and coaches. The final stamp was put on that 2018–2019 edition. And it was final.

The preseason for men's collegiate basketball begins way back in August and is completed in March. It is eight months of commitment, of ups and downs, of wins and losses. And IN THE END, only one team leaves smiling and happy and as a national champ. The college basketball world is known as March Madness in this month of March. There are stunning victories and humbling losses to contend with in March, and when it ends in a loss, it's always bitter.

I had just completed my seventh season as an assistant at VU. In my second year (2013–2014) with the team, we won the NAIA national championship game as we beat Emmanuel College 70–65. In 2019, we lost in the first round. What's it all mean IN THE END?

What it certainly means IN THE END is that the sun will come up the next day, and there will be many sunny tomorrows in life. Again, keep in mind, of the thirty-two teams that make the NAIA tournament and the sixty-eight teams that make the NCAA tournament, only two teams go home as champions. The temporary setback is just that—temporary. Life will go on and become what you make of it.

The guys who played their last college game hopefully embraced the idea in the preceding years that there must be life after basketball. Our team that year had six young men who played their last college game in Kansas City for VU. They gave their hearts and souls to the cause, and I believe they all left a legacy in one form or another. I have no doubts about the successes they will have in future years. May the God of heavens bless each and every one of them richly in the years to come. I'm thankful I got to know those guys, and I thank them for what they did for our Vanguard community. Always remember that what goes around comes around. Work like you don't need the money. Love like you've never been hurt. Dance like nobody is watching. Sing like nobody is listening. And live like it is heaven on earth. Know that God is a BIG GOD—BIG in love, BIG in grace, BIG in favor, BIG in mercy, and BIG in forgiveness. To the seniors that have always played their last game for Vanguard University, I'd like to offer the following words when your time is complete.

IN THE END
By Kevin E. Heenan

IN THE END it's just a simple game,
But it offers so many things.
To me and all the teammates we shared,
We wonder what the years did bring.

In the end it brought perspective,
It brought us wins and bitter defeats.
It brought us tears and smiles and hugs,
And in the end it was complete.

In the end the trials were beaten,
And sweat was wiped from our furrowed brows.
And in the end it was just the beginning,
Of a future that is called now.

In the end it was the lessons learned,
And in the end... it was simply the end.
And now we're hopefully prepared for life,
From foe to time to friend.

In the end we were sad it was finished,
But what awaits us is another day.
And now in this end we have a foundation,
That will lead us on our way.

In the end we are reflective,
And what is done is now complete.
In the end we know how to handle,
Life's victories and defeats.

In the end there were so many lessons,
Ones that we should take to heart.
And now this end is just the beginning,
And this beginning is a brand-new start.

WHO GOD SAYS YOU ARE

One day I wrote about some scriptures I like that provide me with strength to make it through the tough times. Everybody goes through the ups and downs of life, and for me it's nice to read through some bullet-point scriptures that bring me back in touch with God. At these times, I feel like God has this, this life of mine.

Today I was reading up on who God says we are... in another way. We are who God says we are! Once more I've used these ten bullet-point scriptures to remind me of who God says that I am!

GOD SAYS YOU ARE...

MINE — "Do not fear, for I have redeemed you; I have summoned you by name; you are mine" (Isa. 43:1)

PROTECTED — "He will not let your foot slip; He who watched over you will not slumber" (Ps. 121:3).

IMPORTANT — "But you are a chosen people, a royal priesthood, a holy nation, God's special possession, that you may declare the praises of Him who called you out of darkness into His wonderful light" (1 Pet. 2:9).

SPECIAL — "For we are God's handiwork, created in Christ Jesus to do good works, which God prepared in advance for us to do" (Eph. 2:10).

LOVED — "The Lord appeared to us in the past, saying: 'I have loved you with an everlasting love; I have drawn you with unfailing kindness'" (Jer. 31:3).

CREATED WITH PURPOSE — "'For I know the plans I have for you,' declares the Lord, 'plans to prosper you and not to harm you, plans to give you hope and a future'" (Jer. 29:11).

UNIQUE — "For you created my inmost being; you knit me together in my mother's womb" (Ps. 139:13).

EMPOWERED — "I can do all this through Him who gives me strength" (Phil. 4:13).

STRONG — "You make Your saving help my shield, and Your right hand sustains me; Your help has made me great" (Ps. 18:35).

FORGIVEN — "As far as the east if from the west, so far has He removed our transgressions from us" (Ps. 103:12).

I'm glad that God is the one that I need in my life and that He tells me that I am His. I'm glad He tells me that I'm His — protected, important, special, loved, created with a purpose, unique, empowered, strong and forgiven. Amen!

"As for God, His way is perfect; the word of the Lord is flawless. He is a shield for all who take refuge in Him" (2 Sam. 22:31).

YOU'RE THE ONE
By Kevin E. Heenan

You are the air that I breathe,
And You are the only song I can sing.
You're the lamp that lights my path,
You're my Master and my King.

You are the love of my life,
The one who cares so deeply for me.
You're the creator and orchestrator of all,
You're the one who lets me be.

You're the one who provides me unending hope,
The one who gives sight to the blind.
You're the one who can walk upon the water,
I give You my heart, my soul, and my mind.

You're the one who can take my life today,
And You can touch it and make it whole.
You're the Lord over many miracles performed,
You're the only one who can save my soul.

You're the one who stands by the needy ones,
You're the one who can calm any storm.
I want to walk with You every day of the week,
And watch all the miracles that You perform.

Yes, Lord, You're the only one I need,
And You are the only air that I breathe.
Please know, from You I never want to depart,
From You, I never want to leave.

GIVING AND RECEIVING

As an assistant coach I really enjoy being around a team environment. I have been self-employed for over 37 years now as of this writing and there is not the team environment you get when working for yourself. It's always good for my soul to be around a game that has been in my blood since the age of 9. I'm thankful and blessed that I have the opportunity to share basketball with the college players at Vanguard University and I enjoy sharing my thoughts with the players and coaches, some of which are listed below and have been accumulated from my experiences in basketball, business and life. I enjoy being a giver and receiver from my basketball experiences. Some of the things I've learned are:

* When involved in trying times, remember that God didn't do it all in one day. What makes you think you can?

* Usually if someone says to me "You've made my day!" it makes my day.

* That you can always pray for someone when you don't have the finances to help them out or the time to be there for them in times of need.

* That when we pray and ask God for things we should be glad when He doesn't give us everything we ask for.

* People sometimes don't care how much you know until they know how much you care.

* If you ignore the facts it doesn't change the facts.

* You have to surround yourself with people who are more successful and smarter than you are if you want to continue to grow as a person.

* All opportunities are never lost because someone else will take the ones you miss.

* When you harbor bitterness, happiness will dock elsewhere.

* The least expensive way to improve your looks is to simply smile.

* Most people are about as happy as they make their mind up to be.

* Young people need old people's love, respect and knowledge of life and old people need the love, respect, and strength of young people. See, life goes both ways.

* Always leave your loved ones with some loving words or a hug. It could be the last time you ever see them.

* A man at a nursing home told me once that you won't feel your age as long as you keep focusing on your dreams instead of your regrets.

Remembering the little things in life is so important for the happiness of others and us. Let's remember, as Jesus commands us to do, to love others a little more each day, to smile more, to count our blessings, to enjoy our struggles because we're tough enough to make it through with God's help and strength.

"A new command I give you; Love one another. As I have loved you, so you must love one another" (John 13:34).

LET'S REMEMBER
By Kevin E. Heenan

Let's remember that tomorrow is not promised to anyone.

Let's remember to live for today and let the worries of tomorrow take care of themselves.

Let's remember to get off the sidelines of life and get on the playing field.

Let's remember to get after this game of life, which we're blessed with, with each rising sun.

Let's remember to take the extra time to give somebody a smile, a hug, or a kiss.

Let's remember that others are more important than us.

Let's remember that today may be the last chance you get to hold someone tight and tell them you love them.

Let's remember to take time to say "I'm sorry" or "forgive me" or "thank you" or "it's okay."

Let's remember everybody has his or her own faults.

Let's remember to embrace each and every day, and if tomorrow never comes, we'll have no regrets about today.

CAN I PRAY FOR YOU TODAY?

I n my Bible study one morning, I came across the following two verses. These verses got me to thinking about praying for others and whether I should ask other people whom I love how I could possibly pray for their needs and wants.

Galatians 6:2 states, "Carry each other's burdens, and in this way you will fulfill the law of Christ."

Ecclesiastes 4:9–10 states, "Two are better than one, because they have a good return for their labor. If any of them falls down, one can help the other up. But pity anyone who falls and has no one to help them up."

I really don't think God created us to do life alone. We need each other. Somebody in your life that you come in contact with is hurting and wounded. They need your support. They need comfort. They need to know that all is going to be okay.

Friends and relationships will come and go as we move along in life. I met my friend Gary about twenty-five years ago when our children were involved with youth sports. We are still friends but do not talk as much as we did many years ago. We talk maybe six times a year now, as life has a way of moving along, but when we do talk, Gary ALWAYS closes in prayer. It's comforting to know that he believes that carrying our burdens to God in prayer is important. Several months ago, I had a medical procedure that I was going to undergo, and his immediate response was to take it to God in prayer. And he/we did. I felt an immediate sense of relief that God had this. I'm thankful for friends like Gary in my life. I believe God has placed him in my life to encourage me to ask others how I can pray for them.

Let's try to make it a point in the next week to reach out to a few people an d ask them how we can pray for them. There are a lot of people who are hurting in this world and need some love and care—and prayer.

HOW CAN I PRAY FOR YOU?
By Kevin E. Heenan

How can I pray for you?
Tell me what you need.
I'll take your request before my God,
As I pray here from my knees.

I truly trust in the power of prayer,
And I know that you'll receive,
Answers to the questions you have,
Let's pray and just believe.

Offering these prayers to the heavens above,
Is the wisest thing to do.
Because the Lord hears and answers prayers,
In His perfect timing for You.

Expect some miracles in your life,
As we lay your requests before the Lord.
He says He hears all of our prayers,
That none of them are ignored.

It's good to know there's a God who cares,
Do you know He seeks you every day?
He wants you to share your life with Him,
And He listens when you pray.

When I pray for you to the Lord up above,
I know He'll help us with our pleas.
I know He'll answer and I know He'll provide,
The answers that you need.

I know it's a simple question I ask,
But it's something that you should do.
And that's to let me know what you need,
When I ask, how can I pray for you?

IT'S SUPPOSED TO BE HARD

One of my favorite movies of all time is *A League of Their Own*. In one of the scenes, Tom Hanks is talking with his star player who has decided that "it just got too hard." Any manager or coach losing his star would be upset, but his words of wisdom can resonate anytime and anywhere with anybody:

"IT'S SUPPOSED TO BE HARD. IF IT WASN'T HARD, EVERYONE WOULD DO IT. THE HARD IS WHAT MAKES IT GREAT!"

Life is ever evolving and changing. It is a constant surge of twists and turns and ups and downs. Life is a journey, for sure, a steady climb and an uphill battle. Life is filled with surprises, agony, healings, hardships, and celebrations. Life can't be lived with only one emotion written across your heart.

Embrace the hard of life. Lean into it. There are rewards in the trying times of life. Smile when you need to and cry if you have to. Bend but never break, and pick yourself up and make today just about winning, despite the circumstances.

Work and hustle all the time because this is your life. Make the effort to win each day in all you do—your work, relationships, hobbies, games. Don't let anything get in your way. Be determined. Be resourceful. Be aggressive in your dreams. Be on the attack to accomplish your goals and dreams, and let nothing stand in the way, just for today. Know that when you give your all to a dream, at the end of the day, it won't matter how hard it was. Remember, it's supposed to be hard! My poem, IT'S SUPPOSED TO BE HARD is written to players who understand what it takes to get the hard done.

IT'S SUPPOSED TO BE HARD
By Kevin E. Heenan

I'm in the sweat and in the grind,
Because that's a place I don't mind.
Hustling and diving all of the time,
Playing this game that is all mine.

It all comes together when I lace up those shoes,
I'll sacrifice anything so I don't have to lose.
These talents I have I won't misuse,
I'll never have regret or make an excuse.

When it's time to go and it's time to play,
I won't let anything stand in my way.
Before each day I'll stop and I'll pray,
Because I'm giving my all and I'm winning today!

From the get-go I'm wheeling and on the attack,
Playing to win and that's just a fact.
Nothing will keep me from falling off track,
I'm winning today and I'm not looking back.

I'm not looking for the easy way out,
And we all know life is full of negatives and doubts.
But I'm playing to win because that's what I'm about,
And at the end of the day this is what I'll shout:

"The results that I'm seeking will just have to wait,
Because I'm willing to battle each and every day.
One thing I know that covers my plate,
Is that it's the hard that makes everything great."

GOD NEVER CHANGES

Two of my favorite verses from Scripture are listed below, and they relate to the fact that God never changes.

"For I, the Lord, do not change" (Mal. 3:6), and "Jesus Christ is the same yesterday and today and forever" (Heb. 13:8).

Our God never changes. God does not have mood swings. The God of the ages does not move. His knowledge and wisdom will never increase or diminish. He will never be weaker or stronger. Influences that cause change in your life have zero effect on God. IF you cling to Him, His strength will sustain you.

Psalm 33:11 states, "The Lord's plans stand firm forever, His intentions can never be shaken." God has a plan that is unchangeable. It existed at the beginning of time, and it remains today.

God's unchangeable ways assure us of unwavering guidance. Psalm 18:30 states, "As for God, His way is perfect." All the Lord's promises prove true. God's principles for life never change. His guidelines, given in Scripture, produce fruitful lives when you follow them.

God's unchanging Word equips us with timeless truth. Isaiah 40:8 declares, "The grass withers, and the flowers fade, but the word of our God stands forever." God's words and commands are timeless, unchanging, sustaining—forever and ever!

I'LL NEVER CHANGE
By Kevin E. Heenan

When you struggle within, seek My face,
I will lend you My hand and put perspective in place.
Come to Me daily for unlimited gain,
For I'm the Lord Jesus and I'll never change.

I will be there for you, through the thick and the thin,
All you need do is to let Me in.
I will bring you through any storm and provide shelter
from the rain,
For I'm the Lord Jesus and I'll never change.

I do love you dearly, understand that is so,
Trust Me with everything and watch yourself grow.
Give me your everything, the sorrow and pain,
For I'm the Lord Jesus and I'll never change.

I'm the same yesterday, tomorrow, and today,
I want to lead you and keep you from going astray.
I've healed the sick, the blind, and the lame,
For I'm the Lord Jesus and I'll never change.

People are fickle and they'll always let you down,
They'll treat you unfairly and kick you to the ground.
But I'm always there for you, always within range,
For I'm the Lord Jesus and I'll never change.

If you're looking for something that's constant and pure,
Look no further, it's Me who is near.
Just give Me your heart and trust My precious name,
For I'm the Lord Jesus and I'll never change.

AFFIRMATION

One thing we can do better in life is to learn how to affirm others. Whether we are running a business enterprise, coaching in athletics, playing in a team environment, whatever the case may be, we need to learn how to better affirm the players, spouses, bosses, employees, or whoever is on our "team."

"For every time you kick someone in the butt, you better pat them on the back ten times." Or so it's been said. People need encouragement. Everybody needs to be loved. People want to know if they're okay and liked. Everybody likes to and needs to be told "good job," "you look nice," "you're incredible," or "I love you."

Uplifting someone's day and mood is good medicine for the soul, both for you in your positive affirmations and for them in receiving some verbal sweetness. Anything that makes this life a little better for all of us is a good thing.

Here is a small list below of some positive things we can **say** to brighten another's day and some action things we can **do** to try to make somebody's day a little brighter.

THINGS TO **SAY**: "Your smile is contagious." "You're more helpful than you realize." "Your inside is even more beautiful than your outside." "You bring out the best in people." **"Sorry you can't make it; we'll miss your energy."** "Being around you makes everything better." "You inspire me." "You're like a breath of fresh air." "When you make up your mind, nothing stands in your way." **"You're an absolute stud."**

THINGS TO **DO**: Send people thank you notes. Pay for the Starbucks of the person behind you in line; in other words, PAY IT FORWARD. Bring bagels or donuts to the office or team you're on. Leave notes with thoughtful messages on the steering wheel of your partner's car. Hold the door open for people. Let someone cut ahead of you at the grocery store checkout. Have flowers delivered to your mom or a special someone for no reason. Send somebody a text to tell them you're thinking of them. Leave a more-than-generous tip for your server at a restaurant.

The lists can go on and on and on. All it takes is a little effort, a little effort to think of others and what might make them smile or feel good about themselves.

In the same way, I came across a few scriptures today that I feel affirm my belief that God is telling me how important I am to Him and how He promises me things by affirmations through His Word.

PSALM 9:9: The Lord is a refuge for the oppressed, a stronghold in times of trouble.

PSALM 39:7: But now, Lord, what do I look for? My hope is in You.

2 PETER 1:3: His divine power has given us everything we need for a Godly life through our knowledge of Him who called us by His own glory and goodness.

PROVERBS 3:6: In all ways submit to Him and He will make your paths straight.

PHILIPPIANS 4:13: I can do all this through Him who gives me strength.

Let's take a little time this week to make someone's life a little better. Go ahead and fill up your spouse's gas tank. Tell someone they know how to find the silver lining in everything. Tell someone on an elevator that you used to work as an elevator operator but you quit because the job had too many "ups and downs." It's guaranteed to make them smile! Like God makes our days better with the blessings He always provides for us, let's be a similar blessing to somebody else's day. People need to be affirmed. AMEN!

WHAT IF

W HAT IF we woke up today with only what we thanked God for yesterday?

When was the last time we quietly sat and made a list of ALL the blessings we have, from relationships to personal belongings to the food we eat each day and the clothes we wear, AND then we thanked God for it? IF we sit and make a list of all the little things (blessings) we have in life, we might be amazed what we have that we take for granted.

God is always working in our lives even if we feel He is a million miles away. Seeking God is the most exciting and right thing that we can do in life. And the best part of it is, it's a real challenge. Being a follower of Christ is hard. It is not for the faint of heart.

It's a daily challenge to live up to being Christ-like in everything we do. He will always be the great and mighty one. Knowing that it is best to always trust God is easy with intention, but difficult to do and live out. But God will honor our intentions. First Samuel 16:7 says, "But the Lord said to Samuel, 'Do not look on his appearance or on the height of his stature, because I have rejected him. For the Lord sees not as man sees; man looks on the outward appearance, but the Lord looks on the heart.'"

Even if a healing doesn't come and our life falls apart and our dreams are undone, He still is God, forever faithful and forever one. His ways our not our ways, for sure. But He always tenderly loves us, provides for us, and cares for us.

Let's take a look at our blessing list. Let's make it our prayer today to honor, praise, and be thankful for an eternal God who loves us and provides for us, despite when we think He's not around. Let's make it our prayer to have an awareness of the blessings He's provided to us in our lives.

Remember, God didn't promise days without pain, laughter without sorrow, or sun without rain, but He did promise strength for the day, comfort for the tears, and a light for the way. If God brings us to it, He will bring us through it!

"But godliness with contentment is great gain. For we brought nothing into the world, and we can take nothing out of it. But if we have food and clothing, we will be content with that" (1 Tim. 6:6–8).

THOUGHTS ON PRAYER

The purpose of prayer is to bring us to an understanding of the Father's heart. Prayer does not always lead us to an answer that satisfies our wants, desires, and curiosities. Prayer does, however, lead us to a place where we can accept that such answers are unnecessary to involving ourselves in the vast and mysterious purposes of the Father.

P rayer is active and not static. God can handle our everything! He can handle our doubts, our fears, our angers, and our questions. We can bring anything and everything to Him via prayer. Never doubt the power of prayer, because prayer changes everything. The world's greatest wireless connection is prayer, so, let's move forward in our prayer life daily. Prayer is man's greatest power! So, let's not wonder or worry about the significance of our prayers and what God thinks about them. Let's just pray to God and let Him take care of the rest.

A simple prayer for today: Heavenly Father and almighty God, we release our burdens over to You, the ones that You never intended for us to carry. We cast all our cares, worries, and fears upon You. Father God, calm our anxious hearts and quiet our restless spirits, and still the troubling thoughts we have and bless us with the assurance that You are in control always. With open hands and arms, we come to You to carry us through our days this year. We thank You for your promises to sustain us, preserve us, and guard us. Protect our hearts and minds with Your peace, a peace that passes all understanding. Father, may Your will be done in our lives this day, in Your way and Your time. Help us, Father, to know that You are always listening to our words and to our hearts. Help us to seek You each moment of every day that we have. AMEN!

WHEN I PRAY TO YOU
By Kevin E. Heenan

Father above, I have to ask of You,
A question about something I do.
The answer is probably just a simple okay,
But I have to ask You this question, just for today.

Why is it Lord that when I pray to You,
My words seem so vague and sometimes not true?
I pray from my heart, but does the meaning come through?
What do You think Lord when I pray to You?

I wonder sometimes if You think my prayers are to small,
And I wonder sometimes if my prayers mean anything at all.
I know that You hear them, because your word says it's true,
What do You think Lord, when I pray to You?

I try to pray from my heart deep inside me,
Asking Your forgiveness and asking to be free.
I'm always asking for something to help me feel renewed,
What do You think Lord, when I pray to You?

I know You understand me Lord because You're a God of love,
When I offer You my simple prayers to the Heavens above.
So I think I'll keep praying in all that I do,
And not really wonder what You think... when I pray to You.

STORMS OF LIFE

The lighthouse... there is something elusive about it that fascinate many people. Perhaps it's the link to the past and the fact that a lighthouse serves heroic purposes. One of the strongest images of standing strong in a storm is the lighthouse. In eras before radar, navigation, and GPS systems, lighthouses were vital to protect ships from crashing onto rocks, shoals, and shores. Their intention was to simply protect all mariners as they approached rocky shores, and they brought light in the midst of fog or troubled times on the waters of life.

When pilots of the sea were in trouble, the lighthouse was a beacon of hope. When the gray matter or fog of life was evident to sailors and they were threatened with disaster, the lighthouse provided light and hope for safety.

The sea with its waves and unpredictability, its vastness and depths, parallels life itself. The light in the distance parallels our opportunities in life to reach out to the light for direction and guidance. The lighthouse was a light that shined in the darkness, and the lighthouse was simply designed to help those in times of trouble.

Our Christian walk can be compared to being that type of light for those in trouble. In the Gospel of Matthew 5:14–16, Jesus says "You are the light of the world. A town built on a hill cannot be hidden. Neither do people light a lamp and put it under a bowl. Instead they put it on its stand, and it gives light to everyone in the house. In the same way, let your light shine before others, that they may see your good deeds and glorify your Father in heaven."

Lighthouses are constructed and made ready to do their work in the bitterest and harshest conditions, confident that their structure will not crumble when the storms are the fiercest. As Christians, we have to be prepared in our daily battles to live a life pleasing to the Lord in the storms of our lives. He equips us with the foundation of His Word and wraps us with His protective layers of love so we can be a light and a ray of hope constantly. We need to be that hope of His light to everyone. We need to avoid inconsistency, not shining brightly some nights and then dimmed the next. We need to always provide the light and hope to a hurting world.

Life has many struggles, storms, and problems we all have to weather during the seasons of our lives. *Sometimes we just need to bow our heads, say a prayer, and weather the storms*—to outlive them, outdo them, lean into them. We must be willing to fight through them. Sometimes leaning on our God in times like this is crucial. Most of the time, it's the best thing we can do.

There's an old saying I like: **"Life isn't about waiting for the storm to pass.... It's about learning to dance in the rain."** One of the things about life is that there will always be other storms in our lives. It's the way the world works—snowstorms, rainstorms, windstorms, sandstorms, firestorms, you name it. Some are fierce and others are small. You have to deal with each one separately, but you need to keep an eye on what's brewing for tomorrow, maybe all the while searching for the Lighthouse.

Matthew 7:24–27 tells us:

"Therefore everyone who hears these words of mine and puts them into practice is like a wise man who built his house on the rock. The rain came down, the streams rose, and the winds blew and beat against that house; yet it did not fall, because it had its foundation on the rock. But everyone who hears these words of mine and does not put them into practice is like a foolish man who built his house on sand. The rain came down, the streams rose, and the winds blew and beat against that house, and it fell with a great crash."

Let's seek our shelter in God when life's storms come our way. Let us have Christ be our rock.

SHELTER FROM THE STORM
By Kevin E. Heenan

Oh Lord, can You shelter me from the storms,
That the daily grinds of life can bring?
Come walk beside me through the moments of my day,
Over all my life be King.

Some days are cloudy and some days bring rain,
While others are filled with sunshine.
As I feel You cradle me within Your arms,
Is when I see that You're totally divine.

Your presence is something that I must certainly have,
I need You to be near as the days pass on.
You have to walk right beside me every day,
Because to Your love I have been drawn.

My Lord and my God, I can't do it alone,
But I know that You're certainly mine.
It's a relief to know, that when I'm out on the go,
You're there for me every time.

As the storms of my life are calmed by Your touch,
And Your mercy and grace are passed unto me,
I'm thankful for You, God, that You care for me so,
With You in my life, I'm so free.

Amen to You, Lord, You're the Master of all,
As evidenced by all that You've done.
You're the King of all kings and Lord of all lords,
And You're certainly second to none.

THE WINDOW

I wanted to share one of my all-time favorite reads, and it's about encouraging others. It is a slight variation from its original writer, Allan Seager, who published this story under the title "The Street" in *Vanity Fair* magazine in 1934. The original version is included in Seager's 1950 short story collections, *The Old Man of the Mountain and Seventeen Other Stories*.

The title "The Street" has also come to be known by the name "The Window." By either title of the story, it's a nice positive story to share and reads as such:

> Two men, both seriously ill, occupied the same hospital room. One man was allowed to sit up in his bed for an hour each afternoon to help drain the fluid from his lungs. His bed was next to the room's only window. The other man had to spend all his time flat on his back.

> The men talked for hours on end. They spoke of their wives and families, their homes, their jobs, their involvement in the military service, where they had been on vacation.

Every afternoon, when the man in the bed by the window could sit up, he would pass the time by describing to his roommate all the things he could see outside the window. The man in the other bed began to live for those one-hour periods where his world would be broadened and enlivened by all the activity and color of the world outside.

The window overlooked a park with a lovely lake. Ducks and swans played on the water while children sailed their model boats. Young lovers walked arm in arm amidst flowers of every color, and a fine view of the city skyline could be seen in the distance.

As the man by the window described all this in exquisite details, the man on the other side of the room would close his eyes and imagine this picturesque scene.

One warm afternoon, the man by the window described a parade passing by. Although the other man could not hear the band, he could see it in his mind's eye as the gentleman by the window portrayed it with descriptive words. Days, weeks, and months passed.

One morning, the day nurse arrived to bring water for their baths only to find the lifeless body of the man by the window, who had died peacefully in his sleep. She was saddened and called the hospital attendants to take the body away.

As soon as it seemed appropriate, the other man asked if he could be moved next to the window. The nurse was happy to make the switch, and after making sure he was comfortable, she left him alone. Slowly and painfully, he propped himself up on one elbow to take his first look at the real world outside. He strained to slowly turn to look out the window beside the bed. It faced a blank wall.

The man asked the nurse what could have compelled his deceased roommate, who had described such wonderful things outside this window. The nurse responded that the man was blind and could not even see the wall.

She said, "Perhaps he just wanted to encourage you."

Despite our own situations, there is tremendous happiness in making other people happy and feel good about life and their issues. There is a saying "Shared grief is half the sorrow, but happiness when shared is doubled," and that speaks volumes to me and this story. Perhaps the blind man by the window truly felt he was giving solely of himself to his roommate, encouraging him by telling him of all the wonderful things that were happening in his world. He truly was trying his best to brighten another's world.

Encouragement to others is something everyone can give. Somebody needs what you have to give. It may not be your money; it may be your time. It may be your heart. It may be a listening ear. It may be your arms to encourage. It may be your smile to uplift. No one knows for sure, but EVERYBODY can use some encouragement.

It's been said *a word of encouragement during a failure for someone is worth more than an hour of praise after success.* During holiday seasons, when so many people are down on their luck and struggling mightily, let's be aware of our chances to encourage others in love. The list is endless. Maybe it's a coach, a teammate, a teacher, a pastor, a spouse, a friend, a parent, a grandparent, a son, a daughter, a boss, a doctor, a dentist, WHOEVER! This world is in need of encouragement, so let's join together and make a pact to ENCOURAGE others. AMEN!

LISTENING

L ISTEN UP! Is it a coincidence that the word *listen* also contains the same letters as the word *silent*? Is it a coincidence that when God made us, fearfully and wonderfully, Scripture tells us in Psalm 139:14 that He made us ALL with one mouth and two ears? Perhaps the intent of God was to have us listen twice as much as we speak. It reminds me of an old saying, "Listen thrice. Think twice. Speak once."

The great leaders of the past and of today all share one common strength, and that is that they have the incredible ability to LISTEN. They LISTEN and ABSORB what is being said as how it relates to the task at hand. They are not talking the talk as they are walking the walk.

I have found over the years that most people do not listen with the *intent to understand*; rather, they listen with the *intent to REPLY*. To be able to LISTEN to God, we have to slow down and settle in. The world we live in is chaotic and busy. It's important that we STOP and SLOW down and get right and quiet before God so we can hear what He has to say to our hearts.

Most of us are better at talking than listening, but being able to communicate with God involves both. God wants to hear us, and He wants us to hear Him. His goal is for us to understand **HIS** ways. One of the main instruments that God uses to speak to us is through the words of Scripture. As He speaks to us through the Word, we won't hear God speaking to us unless we make *LISTENING* a priority. God does want us to be able to hear Him in both noisy and calm situations. Listening is a critical skill for ensuring that our hearts will be open to His divine guidance. Let's make sure we LISTEN up by being quiet so He can show us how to understand His grace, love, and ways.

Sometimes the only thing needed to help somebody is simply listening to them. Listening is one of the sincerest forms of respect when actually hearing out what another person has to say. It's interesting that the quieter we become, the more we can hear. Begin the practice of the art of listening. Listen twice as much as you speak.

Here are some scriptures pertaining to LISTENING:

PROVERBS 1:5: "Let the wise listen and add to their learning, and let the discerning get guidance."

JAMES 1:19: "My dear brothers and sisters, take note of this: Everyone should be quick to listen, slow to speak and slow to become angry."

PROVERBS 19:20: "Listen to advice and accept discipline, and at the end you will be counted among the wise."

SHOW ME, LORD
By Kevin E. Heenan

Show me Yourself, Lord,
I ask it just for today.
Keep my spirit quiet, Lord,
As I listen to what You say.

Show me Your grace, Lord,
I need to feel it in my heart.
Keep Your promises coming, Lord,
It's what gives me a fresh new start.

Show me Your love, Lord,
So I can keep my spirits high.
Keep my soul refreshed, Lord,
So my life is real and not a lie.

Show me Your ways, Lord,
And help me understand the way it should be.
Keep me on Your lighted path, Lord,
So Your light will shine through me.

YOU ARE WORTHY

D o you think of yourself as a nobody at times? Do you feel unworthy to come before God or even yourself and present your life, your heart, your spirit? Do you know that God uses simple, ordinary people to do the extraordinary in life?

We are all worthy. Sometimes that's a hard truth to swallow when we make mistakes, get lost in our ways, don't reach our goals, and believe the negative things we think. Know that as humans we are built for progress and not perfection. In some way, shape, or form, we are ALWAYS under construction. Leave perfection out of your life and realize that life is a journey, full of some defeats and some victories along the way. Embrace your worthiness, because God believes you're worthy and you are loved by Him. He understands ALL of your imperfections, and yet Isaiah 43:4 tells us, "Because you are precious in my eyes, and honored, and I love you."

There are many stories in Scripture where ordinary people were called by God to do extraordinary things for Him and His kingdom. These people were just common, ordinary people, people like you and me.

MOSES was living in the desert as a total failure as the prince of Egypt when God called him to deliver a nation. GOLIATH was having a good time taunting the Israelites when a teenage shepherd boy named DAVID was used by God to defeat the giant and become king of a nation. PETER would have lived and died the life of a fisherman except that Jesus called him to establish the church. MARY, the mother of Jesus, was a simple teenage girl living in Nazareth when God called her to be the mother of the Messiah. These were all ordinary people who did extraordinary things because they were worthy of it.

The strong have a high sense of self-worth and self-awareness; they don't need the approval of others. They embrace their ordinariness. Life is too short to waste any amount of time on wondering what other people might think about us. What's most important is not what others think of us, but what's important is what our opinion of ourselves is. We're all imperfect, and we are wired for struggle, so we have to stay on top of ourselves and value our potential and God's ability to open doors for us to do the extraordinary. Life is hard; HOWEVER, we are worthy of love and belonging. Despite all of our shortcomings, our pasts, our negative attitudes, our brokenness, our guilt, our confusion, whatever it may be, we need to let God work in our lives because of one simple fact: WE ARE worthy!

I'M WORTHY
By Kevin E. Heenan

In Your eyes I'm worthy,
In Your eyes I'm fine.
In Your eyes I'm loved,
By You for all of time.

In Your hands I'm molded,
In Your hands I'm used.
In Your hands I'm striving,
To do things only for You.

In Your arms I'm lifted up,
In Your arms I am free.
In Your arms I'm being shaped,
To be who You want me to be.

In Your heart I'm cared for,
In Your heart You'll always love me.
In Your heart You want me to know,
That to You I'm always worthy.

LET GO, LET GOD

Have you heard the saying "let go, let God" before? I like to keep things simple, and this short phrase sounds economical in our walk in life and with God. It also sounds so easy to do. Just let go of it and let somebody else handle all the mess of life. It sounds inviting, sounds like the right thing to do, but if only we really knew how to let go.

To let God work in our lives we need to let go of the past, and that is never an easy thing to do. Letting go of the past hurts, fears, mistakes, sins, guilt, anger, and such is difficult at best. However, we have to let go of the past so that God can open doors to our future. God holds the keys to a better future for us. He has something better to offer us than past broken relationships, and He has something greater than our past fears or mistakes.

Let God carry the weight for you. "Come to Me all you who are weary and burdened, and I will give you rest. Take my yoke upon you and learn from me, for I am gentle and humble in heart, and you will find rest for your souls. For my yoke is easy and my burden is light" (Matt. 11:28–30).

We will always struggle hard to hold on to our past, but God says, "Trust Me and let go." We need to free ourselves from our burdens of the past. It's dead weight that will eventually sink us. We need to free ourselves from the burdens that we cannot change. We need to give up the control to God and let Him lead our lives. Release everything from the past that is holding you back. Release the pain, the bitterness, the failures, and the missed opportunities, and embrace the grace and power so that God can move you boldly toward the blessings He has for you.

LET GO, LET GOD
By Kevin E. Heenan

I remember days of past, when I was feeling all alone,
I'd look up toward the heavens, when I was
afraid of the unknown.
My Lord said that all I ever wanted was waiting there for me,
Trust Me with your life, and I will set you free.

I will set you free to live, to do the things you want to do,
Where you'll see Me living in others and living inside of you.
Come to Me who labor, and pray to Me if you will,
Come walk along beside Me and your life will be fulfilled.

I want to walk with you, daily if you can,
Trust Me with your life, for you I've got a plan.
One of hope and love and peace, and joy thrown in too,
Walk with Me forever, each moment you'll feel renewed.

THE BOOK

The Book, the Bible, is outdated. Or so it's been said. It is hard to read. It is difficult to understand. It is trying to live its words. However, it is still the Book. It's our lifeblood as Christians to the way God wants us to live and to get to know Him on a more intimate basis. It's outdated, sure, but it's pertinent to today. It's hard to read, but sometimes it's as if God is speaking only to you and those words from over two thousand years ago are written just for you today. Yes, it's hard to understand, but it transcends cultural phenomena from two thousand years ago to today's environment and the universe in which we live. It is the Book. Get it and read it. Pray through what you don't understand. Ask God to reveal answers from His words. It's amazing how the Book will speak to your trials and tribulations and your victories of today. It's still the number-one-selling book in the world. Amen.

"Blessed is the one who does not walk in step with the wicked or stand in the way that sinners take or sit in the company of mockers, but whose delight is in the law of the Lord, and who meditates on His law day and night" (Ps. 1:1–2).

THE BOOK
By Kevin E. Heenan

Reading over Scripture and keeping gentle thoughts,
About the things You said and did and the special things You taught.
Some mornings Your words just grip me, and they tell me what to do,
And other days they softly say You love me through and through.

There's a special calm to Your words and the instruction that
they give,
It tells me how to treat others and what's the best way to live.
I sometimes don't understand why people say it's out-of-date,
If they read it for themselves, maybe it would end their own debate.

Your words provide a comfort and an insight to the day ahead,
I like to meditate upon Your scripture when I arise or go to bed.
You've revealed Yourself to me in the time I spend with these words,
My days are always so much better
when time with You has occurred.

I want Your book to live through me as I walk and seek Your ways,
I want Your love to encompass me and all I do each day.
Help me live my life through Scripture, plain for others to clearly see,
Because to some I might only be the only Bible they'll ever read.

So, thank You for these words from You and the meaning they impart,
I want Your words so deeply etched right within my heart.
I need your words to live my life as I seek a oneness with You,
My prayer is to live Your book genuinely in all I say and do.

HIS WAYS, OUR WAYS

There is a US Marine Corps story that has been passed down over the years. It's a wonderful story about how God's ways are not our ways. I think we have the hardest time in understanding how and why God works in conjunction with our prayer life. At times we feel confident He hears our requests, and at other times, when we come out on the end of our situation, it's like the story here below. I do like the old saying "Be careful what you pray for, for it might be answered!"

During World War II, a US marine was separated from his unit on a Pacific island. The fighting had been intense, and in the smoke and the crossfire, he had lost touch with his comrades.

Alone in the jungle, he could hear enemy soldiers coming in his direction. Scrambling for cover, he found his way up a high ridge to several small caves in the rock. Quickly he crawled inside one of the caves. Although safe for the moment, he realized that once the enemy soldiers looking for him swept up the ridge, they would quickly search all the caves and he would be found and killed.

As he waited, he prayed: "Lord, if it be Your will, please protect me. Whatever Your will, though, I love You and trust You. Amen."

After praying, he lay quietly listening to the enemy begin to draw close. He thought, "Well, I guess the Lord isn't going to help me out of this one." Then he saw a spider begin to build a web over the front of his cave. As he watched, listening to the enemy searching for him all the while, the spider layered strand after strand of web across the opening of the cave.

"Hah," he thought. "What I need is a brick wall, and what the Lord has sent me is a spiderweb. God does have a sense of humor!" As the enemy drew closer, he watched from the darkness of his hideout and could see them searching one cave after another. As they came to his, he got ready to make his last stand. To his amazement, however, after glancing in the direction of his cave, they moved on. Suddenly he realized that with the spiderweb over the entrance, his cave looked as if no one had entered it for quite a while.

"Lord, forgive me," prayed the young man. "I had forgotten that *in You* a spider's web is stronger than a brick wall."

In You... a spider's web is stronger than a brick wall! Sometimes we pray for things and are truly blessed by God's answers. Other times we pray and God doesn't seem to hear our prayers. As I mentioned above, I'm reminded in this story of what's been said many times concerning ANSWERED prayers: be careful what you pray for because God might answer in unexpected ways.

In prayer it is really helpful to remember that God's ways are not our ways. PRAY ANYWAY! Isaiah 55:8 states, "'For My thoughts are not your thoughts, neither are your ways My ways,' declares the Lord." PRAY ANYWAY! God does answer prayer, so let there be no doubt about that. God will respond to what His people ask. Matthew 7:7 (emphasis added) states, "Ask and it **will** be given to you; seek and you **will** find; knock and the door **will** be opened to you." PRAY ALWAYS!

In closing, remember that no prayer is too big for God to answer. There is no promise too hard for God to fulfill. There is no problem too big for God to solve. There is no disease that God cannot heal. There is no heart that God cannot mend. There is no relationship that God cannot restore. There is no sin that God cannot redeem. There is no bondage that God cannot break. There is no need that God cannot meet. There is no mountain that God cannot move. There is no enemy that God cannot defeat. There is nothing that God cannot do for you. Continue to ask Him in prayer, and keep in mind His ways are perfect.

BRIDGES

I've always loved bridges and how the cables support the bridge.

The long span of the bridges of YOUR life is supported by countless cables called **HABITS, ATTITUDES,** and **DESIRES**. What you do in life depends upon what you are AND what you want. What you get from life depends upon how much you want it, how much you are WILLING to work and plan and cooperate and use your resources. The long span of the BRIDGE OF YOUR LIFE is supported by COUNTLESS CABLES that you are spinning now, and this is why today is such an important day. Make sure that the cables you are building and using for your bridge are strong.

HABITS: It is easier to prevent bad habits than it is to break them. Our habits will either make us or break us. We will become what we repeatedly do. Champions are not just born. Champions are made when they commit themselves to life-changing positive habits. Habits are like a cable: you weave a thread each day and at last you cannot break it.

ATTITUDES: Being involved with coaching basketball, an attitude quote that is one of my all- time favorites is from my high school coach, Coach Nash Rivera, who was fond of saying, "It's not the altitude; it's the ATTITUDE!" Whether you are eighteen years old or sixty years old, your life is always under construction, so put on your hard hat and get to work. Attitude is everything. It governs the way you perceive the world and the way the world perceives you. A positive attitude is everything. You cannot have a positive life with a negative mind. Positive attitudes cause a chain of reaction of positive thoughts, events, and outcomes. A positive attitude is the catalyst and sparks extraordinary results.

DESIRES: Your desire to change must be greater than your desire to be the same. The starting point of all achievement is desire. You should have absolutely no desire to be average. A burning desire is basic to achieving anything beyond the ordinary. Don't downgrade your dream just to fit your reality; better yet, upgrade your conviction to match your desires.

My thought for today revolves around the building of walls and the building of bridges. Walls are built to separate two or more entities, whether it be physically, mentally, or spiritually. These walls can create obstacles. They are built with the intention that they represent the idea of defense, protection, or separation. Bridges, on the other hand, are the opposite of walls in their function. Bridges are built to bring together, to join two or more entities, and to create unity. They are built to overcome obstacles.

How does the bridge you're building today in your walk with God look? Are the cables of faith you're erecting in your life ones that are going to be stable and allow you to further your life mission? Is your bridge built of wood or stone or steel? Is your bridge a small one or a massive one? Whatever the bridge you're building, they all provide the same purpose: to get from one side to the other. Your bridge makes it possible to get from point A to point B on the other side of the chasm.

As we build our faith bridge to God, let's do it with gusto, knowing that at the end of our journey, God's loving arms await us. Let's build and develop positive habits, attitudes, and desires toward one another and create more unity in loving others as we build our bridge to God. Know that God will meet us in the middle at any time or any place, as He will honor our attempts to build a relationship with Him.

THE BRIDGE
By Kevin E. Heenan

God, I hear You calling now,
You're telling me to create,
A bridge that's strong and sturdy,
That leads to Your heavenly gates.

The roads I'm traveling on need work,
They're forever on the mend.
I'll build this bridge for all my life,
And at heaven's doors it will end.

Supply my bridge with strength and love,
And a structure that will never sway.
My lifelong goal is to get to You,
At the end of all my days.

I ask that You help me build my bridge,
May it be made from a heart that's true.
And is it possible to meet You halfway,
As I build this bridge from me to You?

PREPARATION

The word for the day is PREPARATION, preparing for today and for the future—the immediate future, the midrange future, and the long-term future. WE MUST BE PREPARED. Many people will say that when someone achieves something in their life, he or she was simply lucky. My belief—and I've seen it countless times—luck is what happens when preparation meets opportunity.

If you fail to prepare for anything in life—be it making a team, staying on the team, passing a test, finding the right vocation or life partner, whatever it might be—if you fail to prepare, you're preparing to fail!

One of my hobbies and passions is cooking. I love to experiment with different recipes; however, I like the ones that have the fewest ingredients and taste the best. Similar to my cooking passions, my recipe for preparation involves only two ingredients, and they have to be married together as one.

The FIRST INGREDIENT is hard work. It is the spice of the recipe, and without hard work, your venture is doomed. This ingredient is also deceiving to the overall plan, as most people think that if they work hard at something, they should be entitled to success. That is not true. Please remember that WORKING HARD goes with the territory. YOU'RE SUPPOSED TO WORK HARD at anything you do in life. It's a given. You show up and work hard. If you don't work hard, it's over. You're done. Somebody is always willing to outwork you.

The SECOND INGREDIENT is the one that is overlooked by most, and that ingredient is the ability to THINK. In addition to working hard, you have to have a plan on how you're going to be successful and work SMART. You have to map out a plan, and in mapping this out, you will have to adjust the sails several times during the course of your voyage. This ingredient is tied closely to writing out your goals on paper and then being prepared to change the game plan while continually working hard in the process.

The following story tells of a young man who worked hard but didn't necessarily have his thinking cap on:

> There was a young man who approached the foreman of a logging crew and asked for a job. The foreman replied, "Let's see you bring this tree down." The young man stepped forward and skillfully felled a great tree. The foreman was impressed and told him, "You can start on Monday."

> Monday, Tuesday, Wednesday, and Thursday came and went; however, on Thursday afternoon, the foreman approached the young man and said, "You can pick up your paycheck on the way out today."

The young man was startled and replied, "I thought you paid on Friday?"

"Normally we do," said the foreman. "But we're letting you go today because you've fallen behind. Our daily charts show that you've dropped from first place on Monday to last place today."

The young man objected, "But I'm a hard worker; I arrive first, leave last, and even have worked through my coffee breaks!"

Sensing the young man's integrity, the foreman then asked "Have you been sharpening your axe?"

The young man replied, "No, sir. I've been working too hard to take time for that!"

The missing ingredient here in this simple story is that although working hard, the young man forgot about doing probably the most important thing in his gig, and that was to keep his axe sharp.

In closing, it's necessary to PREPARE for any endeavor in life. Keep in mind that we are all looking for success, and most people are looking for the easy path to success. Let me clue you in—there is no easy path. Know that success comes in life by GETTING and BEING PREPARED. Like a pregame scout, it will tell you the opponent's strengths and weaknesses. Write up your game plan today as you PREPARE for the seasons of your life, remembering that "IF IT'S TO BE, IT'S UP TO ME!"

DREAMS
By Kevin E. Heenan

Reach high for your dreams,
As far as you can stretch.
Don't ever stop believing in them,
Even in your dying breath.

Others will sometimes tell you,
That your dreams will never come true,
But you just go on about getting them,
Keep striving until your days are through.

Believe in yourself always,
For God will provide that power within.
To accomplish anything you ever want,
Just believe in yourself and begin.

The sidelines of life are littered,
With people who'll try to prove you wrong.
Telling you your dreams won't come true,
So never take those people along.

We are all handed one life to live,
So we must strive to always be best.
Have your preparation always be the top priority,
And the Lord will take care of the rest.

YESTERDAY, TODAY, AND TOMORROW

Today's thoughts bring me to what we think about, what we worry about, and what we're going to do about it. I really like how in the book of Matthew, chapter six, verses 25 through 34, it tells us how to live. And that is without worry. It's with knowing that God has us fed and clothed. I like how verse 34 tells us that each day, the one we're living today, has enough problems of its own. In other words, enjoy today and its battles, and stay in the moment and don't get too far ahead of yourself.

Matthew 6:25–34 (emphasis added):

> Therefore I tell you, do not worry about your life, what you will eat or drink; or about your body, what you will wear. Is not life more than food, and the body more than clothes? Look at the birds of the air; they do not sow or reap or store away in barns, and yet your heavenly Father feeds them. Are you not much more valuable than they? Can any one of you by worrying add a single hour to your life? And why do you worry about clothes? See how the flowers of the field grow. They do not labor or spin. Yet I tell you that not even Solomon in all his splendor was dressed like one of these. If that

is how God clothes the grass of the field, which is here today and tomorrow is thrown into the fire, will He not much more clothe you—you of little faith? So do not worry, saying, "What shall we eat?" or "What shall we drink?" or "What shall we wear?" For the pagans run after all these things, and your heavenly Father knows that you need them. But seek first His kingdom and His righteousness, and all these things will be given to you as well. Therefore do not worry about tomorrow, for tomorrow will worry about itself. Each day has enough trouble of its own.

Jesus does not want us to be anxious and full of worry. He wants us to live life in a different manner. He does not want us making decisions based on a fear of the future. He wants the direction of our lives established on eternal truths rather than temporal things of earth and the hollow promises of man. Jesus is not saying that we can quit working because God will provide. He is saying that we do not have to be anxious because God will provide. Amen to that!

YESTERDAY, TODAY, TOMORROW
By Kevin E. Heenan

Yesterday has me feeling sad and blue,
And today I wonder what might be true.
The tomorrows will always have their point of view,
But this moment I'm only depending on You.

Of yesterday I'm never so sure,
And today I wonder what I'll have to endure.
The tomorrows sometimes leave me feeling insecure,
But this moment that I'm living I'm depending on You.

Yesterday leaves me feeling up in the air,
And today is just hard enough to bear.
Though the tomorrows might just be as unfair,
So this moment I'm offering You all my prayers.

Yesterday isn't as bad as it appears,
And today is just another day in the year.
Hopefully tomorrow won't bring me any tears,
But in this moment I know that You're always near.

Yesterday has passed as finished art,
And today is a day I'll live with all my heart.
In the tomorrows I want You to never depart,
Because in this moment we'll never be apart.

Oh yesterday, you've come and now you have gone,
And today I'm simply trying to get along.
It's to the tomorrows I'll probably be drawn,
But with You in this moment is where I belong.

SEEKING THEE

H ere are some of my favorite verses from the Bible regarding SEEKING God:

"But if from there you seek the Lord your God, you will find Him if you look for Him with all your heart and with all your soul" (Deut. 4:29).

"And you, my son Solomon, acknowledge the God of your father, and serve Him with wholehearted devotion and with a willing mind, for the Lord searches every heart and understands every motive behind the thoughts. If you seek Him, He will be found by you; but if you forsake Him, He will reject you forever" (1 Chron. 28:9).

"But seek first His kingdom and His righteousness, and all these things will be given to you as well" (Matt. 6:33).

"I seek You with all my heart; do not let me stray from Your commands" (Ps. 119:10).

"Seek the Lord while He may be found; call on Him while He is near" (Isa. 55:6).

"Seek the Lord while He may be found." Those are smart words of wisdom. Let's not take our time for granted here on earth, and let's use our time wisely in seeking out God. Scripture says if we seek Him, He will find us. What a great promise! Let's promise ourselves today to seek God with all our heart, all our mind, and all our strength.

SEEKING THEE
By Kevin E. Heenan

Jesus, sweet Jesus, we're glad You're only a prayer away,
And the answers to those prayers just might be answered today.
However, we're just going to seek You with all we have to give,
Because You've told us, Lord, that's the way to live.

We want to be in harmony with You as our day is to begin,
We know You're the answer to all the problems
we have deep within.
You said You were the way, the truth, and the life,
And by turning it all over to You, it will lessen all the strife.

Life can be so complicated and sometimes hard to understand,
But the Lord has clearly said for us He has a plan.
It's up to us to seek Him through every moment of the day,
Like Jesus once said, "I am the truth, the life, and the way."

Heaven's only a prayer away and the Lord will listen well,
He wants us to be forgiven and to spare us all from hell.
Jesus, sweet Jesus, we're so glad You're never far away,
Gently place Your calm upon us and help us hear what You say.

We offer You our lives, Lord, we're precious clay for You to mold,
Bless us with Your power, make us courageous, make us bold.
And as we move forward through this day, bless it abundantly,
And remember, Lord, we're trying, we're trying to seek Thee.

GOD IS THE ONE

"As for God, His way is perfect; the word of the Lord is flawless. He is a shield for all who take refuge in Him" (2 Samuel 22:31).

"The lord lives! Praise be to my rock. Exalted be God, the Rock, my Savior" (2 Samuel 22:47).

God's way is perfect for me. As I strive to please Him every day, I come to recognize that He is literally the air that I breathe. His love for me is all-encompassing, and it is He that I try to strive and live for every day. Lots of times I come up short in my quest to please Him; however, it is nice to know that God will always accept me back into His fold. Amen for that!

MY HOLY GOD
By Kevin E. Heenan

Forgiving, loving, caring and there,
Comforting, joyful, burdens You bear.
Dependable, quiet, gentle with grace,
Peaceful and merciful, You're everyplace.

Strong, powerful and maker of all,
Soothing, tolerant, someone I adore.
Affectionate, friendly, loyal to me,
Master, King, You've set me free.

Kindness, contentment, rest for the soul,
Inspirational, beautiful, You make me whole.
Savior, Lord, always there for the call,
Holy, Heavenly, God above all.

Sturdy, rock-like, in all that You do,
Trusting, giving, provider who's true.
Willing, able, lending Your hand,
Blessed, Redeemer, You're all that I have.

A PRAYER FOR YOU

A close friend of mine had texted me and asked me to say a prayer for him, as he was undergoing a medical procedure that was for a condition that could end up being quite serious. I immediately sat down and wrote the following for him directly from my heart. I wanted him to know that God had him covered and was going to shoulder all his burdens for today and for always. Prayer is sometimes the only thing that you can do for another. Amen.

TODAY'S PRAYER
By Kevin E. Heenan

Today I'll be thinking thoughts of you,
And offering for you my prayers to the heavens above.
Asking that there will be peace granted to you,
And that your heart will be content and full of love.

The trials of the day may seem hard and gray,
And the passing of time may be restless and long.
But one thing is certain as your day goes on,
I'll be praying for you until the sun goes down.

I'll be praying that your day is full of comfort and peace,
And that God's calm will blanket your soul.
I'll pray that you'll be blessed with clarity and hope,
And I'll be praying that our Lord will make you whole.

When you feel fretful, stressed, or unnerved,
Remember that the God of the heavens is certainly there.
Just release your day to Him, let Him be in control,
And He'll shoulder all the burdens you bear.

Because you're special to me, always and today,
I'll be on my knees offering prayers up for only you.
Asking God to provide you with His perfect peace,
Asking God to be with you all the day through.

YOUR EYES

Keep your eyes on Jesus, who both began and finished this race we're in. Study how He did it. He never lost sight of where He was headed—that exhilarating finish in and with God. He could put up with anything along the way: cross, shame, whatever. And now He's there, in the place of honor, right alongside God.

YOUR EYES
By Kevin E. Heenan

Keep Your eyes on me, oh Lord,
And keep Your love within my heart.
Don't let my mind stray away today,
I want us to never be apart.

Take away the defeat that I have,
Shed Your eternal light on my soul.
Help me to soar on eagle's wings,
Make me perfect and make me whole.

Increase my awareness of Your grace,
Let me hear what You have to say.
My God, my God, I am all Yours,
Do what You will with me today.

Your treasures to give are infinite,
I thank You for those gifts I seek.
I want to walk with Your grace today,
And keep me contrite and humble and meek.

Thank You, Lord, for all You've done,
And thank You for my blessings of past.
My walk with You is important to me,
It's something I want to always last.

Oh God, come to the deepest parts of my soul,
And fill me with Your unending love.
Please know I desire to be in communion with You,
As you keep Your eyes on me from above.

TAKE AWAY

Sometimes it's needed to ask God to take away our anger, our fears, and our negative destructive thought patterns to have Him be able to work in us and through us. In Isaiah 58:11, it says, "The Lord will guide you always; He will satisfy your needs in a sun-scorched land and will strengthen your frame. You will be like a well-watered garden, like a spring whose waters never fail."

TAKE AWAY
By Kevin E. Heenan

Take away the anger and the fear,
Replace my anxieties with joy and cheer.
Take away the deceit and the lies,
My goal is to serve You 'til the day I die.

Take away the lust and the needs,
Replace my doubts as You take the lead.
Take away the envy and the shame,
My desire is to praise Your holy name.

Take away the deception and the pride,
As I come to Your arms, open and wide.
Take away the stress and the daily strife,
My want is to give You all of my life.

Take away the wrath and the rage,
It's with You, Lord, I want to engage.
Take away the wants and the greed,
You're all that I want, as You satisfy my needs.

CONTENTMENT

"But godliness with contentment is great gain. For we brought nothing into the world, and we can take nothing out of it" (1 Tim. 6:6–7).

As we continue to live our lives, it's always nice from time to time to just stop and take a look at the blessings we have in our lives—to number them, to take notice of them, to cherish them, and to be thankful for them. In addition to 1 Timothy 6:6–7, there are a couple of other verses in Scripture that tell us about contentment: "I know what it is to be in need, and I know what it is to have plenty. I have learned the secret of being content in any and every situation, whether well fed or hungry, whether living in plenty or in want" (Phil. 4:12). And, "Enjoy what you have rather than desiring what you don't have. Just dreaming about nice things is meaningless—like chasing the wind" (Eccles. 6:9).

Godliness WITH contentment is great gain. As we are numbering our days in this thing called life, and we pause our pursuit for the things of this life, let's take a moment to be thankful for the blessings that we have.

Be thankful for what you have. It will make you content. And when you find contentment with your life, you'll find happiness.

CONTENTMENT
By Kevin E. Heenan

The day laid out before me,
As I walk this sandy shore.
A checklist of the blessings I have,
Reveals I need nothing more.

Be content with what you have,
And give thanks for the day ahead.
For God is certainly watching over you,
Toward His kingdom you're being led.

Live in the moment as you cherish today,
And press on to serve others as you go.
The treasures of life are abundant,
And they come to life by the seeds you sow.

So as I walk this sandy shore,
And be thankful for what's called today.
I'll strive to see God's love for me,
And seek His light, His truth, and ways.

COMING BACK TO GOD

I t's good to know that we have a loving God who will always take us back into His arms when we fail or fall short in whatever we do. Scripture promises IF we hope in the Lord, then our strength will be renewed. What a great promise! As we commit to coming back to You, Lord, thank You for helping us get our feet on the ground, for helping us to get stronger and to soar to unbelievable heights.

"But those who hope in the Lord will renew their strength. They will soar on wings like eagles; they will run and not grow weary, they will walk and not be faint" (Isa. 40:31).

COMING BACK
By Kevin E. Heenan

I'm coming back to You, Lord,
Coming back to You today.
I'm throwing away the defeats I've had,
And I'm going to listen for what You say.

I'm giving You my cares and worries,
That consume my every thought.

I want to seek and find and try to live,
The precious things You taught.

I want a setting sun on my days of past,
I want future days with You by my side.
No longer am I going this life alone,
Once again You'll be my only guide.

Why do I do my days with wonder and worry?
When I know You're available to pull me through.
I'm starting over in seeking You,
In all I think and say and do.

As I go today, please come beside me,
Help me feel Your presence here.
Bless me with a special longing,
That wants to hold You close and near.

Make a pathway for the steps I walk,
Light my way that leads to heaven's doors.
I only want to fly home to You,
Take my wings and help me soar.

Thank You, Lord, for taking me,
Back to Your arms of love.
Where I'm sheltered, protected, and cared for,
By You, from the heavens high above.

BEING A CHAMPION

E verybody wants to be a champion, but not everybody wants to put in the necessary work to become one. You have to develop a plan in becoming a champion, and the first step is the desire to become one, to start to think like a champion IN ALL AREAS OF YOUR LIFE. Why? It's because there is carryover in all aspects of life in becoming a champion. IF you don't go to class and instead rest for your athletic endeavor, well, you just cheated yourself out of becoming a total champion in life. Sure, you'll be rested for your activity, but you cheated some-where else in your existence. That is not good. Champions are champions in ALL areas of their lives—the classes they take, the sport they play, the relationships they encounter.

In closing, Hebrew 12:1–3 (emphasis added) tells us: Therefore, since we are surrounded by such a great cloud of witnesses, let us throw off everything that hinders and the sin that so easily entangles. And LET US RUN WITH PERSEVERANCE THE RACE MARKED OUT FOR US, fixing our eyes on Jesus, the pioneer and perfecter of faith. For the joy set before Him He endured the cross, scorning its shame, and sat down at the right hand of the throne of God. Consider Him who endured such opposition from sinners, so that you will not grow weary and lose heart.

BE A CHAMPION
By Kevin E. Heenan

What kind of champion are you going to be today?
One who comes to fight or one who runs the other away?
A champion is one who fights to the very end,
And never gives up and never gives in.

The seasons of life will always be moving forward,
And the question at the end is, did you give it your all?
So give of yourself with all your blood and sweat,
Because at the end of it all, you want zero regrets.

Life is so fleeting so you must have that goal,
To have that champion's heart against any and all foes.
Champions look forward to winning every play,
And not for a one-time thing, but day after day after day.

The day you decide to be a champ and not a chump,
Is that first day that will get you over the hump.
At the end of the day and when you lay your head to rest,
A champion knows in his heart that he did his best.

True champions deal with adversity and always bounce back,
Desire and toughness are something they don't lack.
A champion is always prepared and always on guard,
Because being a champion is something that's hard.

The quest to be a champion has long winding roads,
With twists and turns and the heaviest of loads.
Becoming a champion is hard but can be done,
A champion question for you is, can you be one?

BEING STILL BEFORE GOD

"BE STILL, AND KNOW THAT I AM GOD" (PS. 46:10).

Heavenly Father, help us today to just be still—to be quiet, to pause before we speak, to be ready to listen to Your still voice. Help us see the good in others as we seek the good and the God in You. Help us to BE STILL in the hustle and bustle of the world in which we live. Quiet our souls so we can love. Quiet our minds so we can reflect. Quiet our hearts so we can hear You and only You.

BE STILL
By Kevin E. Heenan

__BE STILL__, and know that I am your God,
Know that I am with you at all times.
I will lessen your burdens and help you along,
My gentle voice will show you what is right and what is wrong.

__BE STILL__, and know that I am your God,
That I watch over you, I always see what you do.
I will answer your prayers that you offer to Me,
Be persistent in asking, and the blessings you'll see.

BE STILL, *and know that I am your God,*
That I will lead you out of the valleys of darkness.
Know when you're down and troubled, I'm right by your side,
Protecting you from life's strong rushing tides.

BE STILL, *and know that I am your God,*
And in your loneliness I stand holding you in my arms.
Nothing in this world could ever get the best of you,
Because you're wrapped in My love, a love that is true.

BE STILL, *and know that I am your God,*
If you seek Me daily, you will find the plan for your life.
When you live your life to please Me, My blessings abound,
You'll hear that heaven's music for your life is a beautiful sound.

BE STILL, *and know that I am your God,*
And know that nothing is impossible with Me.
Offer to Me your complete heart and soul,
Surrender yourself and I'll make your life whole.

BE STILL, *and know that I am your God,*
And that I desire a total oneness with you.
Continually seek after Me, day after day,
This oneness with Me is the only way.

BEING HUMBLE

"DO NOTHING FROM SELFISHNESS OR EMPTY CONCEIT, BUT WITH HUMILITY OF MIND LET EACH OF YOU REGARD ONE ANOTHER AS MORE IMPORTANT THAN HIMSELF" (PHIL. 2:3).

Dear God, help us today to see that others are truly more important than ourselves. This world that You created isn't just about us. Help us to put aside our selfishness and give to others what You've given so freely to us—simply LOVE, and layers and layers of LOVE. Help us today to live simply, to love generously, to care deeply, and to speak kindly. As we humble ourselves before You, we'll just leave this special day in Your hands.

HUMBLE YOURSELF
By Kevin E. Heenan

I must humble myself to You to obtain that perfect peace,
That place where I'm less known, that place where You increase.
I humble myself before You now, knowing You're the only ne,
Who provides for my every day, my God who is second to none.

With You in the lead of my life, my days are so much better,
I can offer You my burdens and cares for You to only weather.
I simply can't live a day of my life without You in control,
I need to submit to You fully, my heart, my mind, and soul.

When I'm right with You, I feel the fruits that make my spirit whole,
Love, joy, peace, and gentleness filling up my soul.
But away from You and out walking where me is all I see,
I get filled up with anger and selfishness, hatred and envy.

Pride always goes before destruction, it precedes any man's fall,
And if you get in this position, back to the Lord you must crawl.
Humble yourself before Him, let Him know
you're willing to cease,

And get back to the place where God is on the increase.
Father, go before me now, walk ahead of me if You will,
And throughout the days I live, help me listen and be still.
I want to hear Your gentle voice again telling me to follow You,
I humbly come before You now, seeking You in all I do.

DOING IT WELL

His Master replied, "Well done good and faithful servant"
(Matt. 25:21).

L IFE can be frustrating. There are many books and maga-
zines and websites telling us all how to be successful, no
matter what the topic might be. Whether it comes to parenting,
being a spouse, coworkers, losing weight, whatever the topic,
there are limitless articles and opinions on how to do it all per-
fectly. The other day I was looking for the perfect rib recipe,
so I typed into YouTube's search engine "PERFECT baby back
ribs," and it came up with 99,300 different ways. Wow! Really?
So many "perfects" for just one recipe! It made me realize there
might be a lot of "perfects" in making baby back ribs, but we
are certainly not perfect as humans. I'll just try in my own
imperfections to honor the scripture from 1 Corinthians 10:31
that states, "So whether you eat or drink or whatever you do, do
it all for the glory of God." I just hope and pray that at the end
of the day, I can lie in bed and thank God for the day, knowing
that I gave Him my best, despite whatever failures I might have
had in the day. I just want Him to whisper to me at the end of
the day, "Well done, good and faithful servant."

WELL DONE, GOOD AND FAITHFUL SERVANT

By Kevin E. Heenan

I have a soft yet gentle spirit,
One that prefers peace and no pain.
But in the anguish of my days, oh Lord,
I sometimes wonder what I've gained.

I think back to the time I committed to You,
When I opened that door for You to come in.
It was understood that I would begin a new life,
And that You had entered my heart and washed away my sin.

I sometimes find the walk to be hard,
And at times like I've completely let You down.
I find myself praying and asking of You,
Could You please just lift my hopes up off the ground?

I just want to please You and be committed to You,
And my desire is to trust You in all that I do.
Because I know Your love is unconditional,
And I feel Your grace through and through.

But am I a Christian who does good work for You?
And one who serves Your kingdom with fervor,
I just want you to say at the end of it all,
"WELL DONE, GOOD AND FAITHFUL SERVANT."

THOUGHTS TO PONDER

Inspiring one-liners are something that I've found over the years to be a good source of motivation and a good source of quick reflection about life and people. During our trying times and during our times of victory, keeping ahead of the game of life is always a challenge. IF you're a professing Christian, see if some of these one-liners can help you ponder our place with God and each other.

IF you want to convince others of the value of Christianity...live it!

A genuine Christian is the best evidence of the genuineness of Christianity.

IF you want to defend Christianity, then practice it.

A Christian must get on his knees before he gets on his feet.

Christians may not see eye to eye, but they can walk arm in arm.

The cross is easier to the Christian who picks it up and carries it than to the one who just drags it along.

An idle Christian is the raw material of which backsliders are made.

Christians are kind of like pianos... grand, square, upright, and no good unless in tune.

God is not only a present help in time of trouble, but also a great help in keeping us out of trouble.

Some Christians wish to be counted in, but not to be counted on.

No garment is more becoming to a Christian than the cloak of humility.

Dear Lord, professing to be a Christian is risky business because when we fail, it makes You look like You're not real to a world that constantly will judge us in the light of only perfection. Thank You for forgiving us when we fail. Thank You for putting us back on track to pleasing You when we don't come through for You. Thank You for always being there for us when we fail You. Know that we ache and hurt when we disappoint You and let You down. Thank You for Your love, Your direction, Your forgiveness, and Your hope. Amen.

ACHING AND HURTING
By Kevin E. Heenan

Oh Lord, I'm aching and hurting today,
Just thought You might want to know.
The winter winds have chilled my soul,
Why must these strong bitter winds blow?

I'm relieved Your mercy endures forever,
And Your love for us will never cease.
It is said that the one whose mind is fixed on You,
Has been promised to be kept in perfect peace.

Oh Lord, what a refuge we have in You,
Where You provide us shelter from the storms.
To be delivered into the arms of almighty God,
Where we're taken in when feeling alone.

Sometimes the days we live in are rough,
But when we turn to You, You calm the storm.
I know You can walk upon the waters of my life,
And turn my cold days back to warm.

The aches and hurts from this day will certainly pass,
And I'm asking You, Lord, to reveal me my gain.
And as I turn my thoughts to what You did on that cross,
I realize how minimal is my pain.

WORK IN MY LIFE, LORD

T here are days when we need to just depend on God's leading. Life is just flat-out tough sometimes, and we need to find our will and resolve to JUST trust God FULLY at these times. What's the saying? "It's easier said than done." But there's another saying I really like, and it's "Let's just remember that when all is said and done, that more is done than said." Amen to that. Let's glorify our true Redeemer in all circumstances and look forward to the blessings that come from our tough times. While we're in this world, we need to be the light.

"As long as it is day, we must do the work of Him who sent Me. Night is coming, when no one can work. While I am in the world, I am the light of the world" (John 9:4–5).

WORK IN MY LIFE, LORD
By Kevin E. Heenan

I need You to work in my life, Lord,
So that I can become more precious like You.
And maybe others can see Your light shining,
In what I say and do.

I've failed so miserably in the past, Lord,
Forgive me for my neglectful ways.
I've never provided Your light to anyone, Lord,
I've stayed in darkness most of my days.

Could You find the time to come to me,
And mold me from this place that I'm in?
There's no way that I can do it alone, God,
Please reshape me and begin from within.

I feel so bad for all the many times,
That I've failed to live my life for You.
But as I ask You this morning to forgive me,
Help me move forward and show me what You can do.

Let's see if we can shine Your light, Lord,
On those who have no hope and are down.
Let's see if we can help them along, Lord,
To move them forward as we help them from the ground.

The prayer that we will offer together,
Is a prayer that Your angels will hear.
We will ask for and thank You for Your forgiveness,
And we will hold Your mercy so dear.

Oh Lord, I thank You for the time,
Again, as You've listened to someone like me.
Please know that I love You so much,
And that's the way that I want it to be.

THE GOD OF THE SECOND CHANCE

O ur relationship with God changes daily, in my opinion, and only does so because we are human. With humanity come many good qualities, but also some not so good. I find that the God that I pray to and honor offers me second and millionth chances all at once. I'm always in need of another chance with God as I stumble in my walk. Praise God that He's always there for us.

God is not only the God of second chances; He is the God of another chance, and another chance, and another chance. This is good news because most of us mess up the second chance fairly quickly. One of the amazing facets of God's character is His incredible patience with us. Psalm 86:15 says it well: "But you, O Lord, are a God merciful and gracious, slow to anger and abounding in steadfast love and faithfulness." Micah 7:18 says, "Who is a God like you, pardoning iniquity and passing over transgression for the remnant of his inheritance? He does not retain his anger forever, because he delights in steadfast love."

The Bible is full of people who received second chances, and even third and fourth chances: Peter, Jonah, Mark, Samson, David, and others. All are trophies of God's grace.

Just as God is patient and forgiving, He wants His children to be patient with and forgiving of others. "Therefore, as God's chosen people, holy and dearly loved, clothe yourselves with compassion, kindness, humility, gentleness and patience" (Col. 3:12). He gives us second chances, and we must give the same to others. Jesus gives a stern warning to those who refuse to forgive, saying that if we will not forgive others, God will not forgive us (Matt. 6:15; see also Eph. 4:32; Col. 3:13; and Prov. 19:11). If someone is truly repentant, then we are obligated to forgive (Matt. 18:21–22).

Forgiveness, however, is not the same thing as reconciliation. Many people struggle to find the balance between showing mercy and enabling a harmful person to continue harming. We should forgive everyone who wrongs us, just as Jesus forgives us. Forgiveness is between our heart and God's, removing any barriers that unforgiveness brings. When someone continues to unrepentantly violate another person's boundaries, a wise person learns to set firmer boundaries. If a man has repeatedly punched you in the face, you can forgive him, but you don't stand within arm's distance until he has proved over time that he has changed.

Giving someone a second chance means we give him another chance to earn our trust. But that does not mean we instantly forget what experience has taught us. Trust must be earned over time, and we are foolish if we give trust prematurely. We can have a loving and forgiving heart that also practices wise guardianship over our lives.

When we have wronged someone, we have no right to demand another chance. But we should work to earn another chance by continued demonstration of repentance and change.

There may come a time in a human relationship when the same thing has occurred, when forgiveness has been offered and restoration made possible, but one party refuses to repent and rejects all efforts to reconcile. It may be time to end that relationship. Second chances are no longer working. Ending a relationship is a last resort, but sometimes it must be done (Matt. 18:17).

God does everything possible to draw us to repentance, offering forgiveness and second chances (2 Pet. 3:9). But if we continue to reject Him, the offer is withdrawn, and at death there are no more chances (Heb. 9:27). God's grace is our model.

THE GOD OF THE SECOND CHANCE
By Kevin E. Heenan

I'm thankful that I know a loving God,
Someone who cares and is always there for me.
And as time goes by and my days are further advanced,
I see and realize, You're the God of the second chance.

Your forgiveness and Your mercy are always there,
For me to experience and always have.
I realize that this life I live is my song and dance,
And I can't do it without my God, who's the author
of the second chance.

Mistakes of my past are easily wiped away,
By repenting and turning back to Your will.
My sins of the past forgiven, never once given a second glance,
By You, the God of the second chance.

Being cradled in Your arms when my weary soul needs rest,
Is a comfort I've come to know when I pray to You.
My life is so much better when with You I have a stance,
A stance that offers stability, with the
God of the second chance.

Your tireless love You demonstrate toward me,
Provides me with the comfort and strength I need.
Lord, I just want You to know that my life is enhanced,
When I'm near You, my God of the second chance.

THE SAINT WHO ADVANCES ON HIS KNEES NEVER RETREATS

A *saint* is a term or word used for somebody who is recognized as having a high degree of holiness or likeness to God. In Christian circles, it entails any believer who is "in Christ" and in whom Christ dwells, whether in heaven or on earth. I want to keep the word's definition in a loose fashion for the moment, because we all know that in our human weaknesses, we all fall short of God's standards on a daily basis. However, in our quest to become more like God in our thoughts and actions, sometimes we can see the result of being "saint-like," in laymen's terms.

The beginning of the phrase THE SAINT WHO ADVANCES ON HIS KNEES NEVER RETREATS gives me the thought that IF you are truly praying your way through each moment of each day and year that you live, you are going to be in God's blessings and you are going to be seeking His will for your life and those around you.

We've got to get on our knees and pray to God. Prayer is what advances us. It allows us to keep in constant communication with our creator. If we do not move deeper into our fellowship with Him through prayer, we retreat from fellowship with

Him. Prayer is active, not static. You cannot stand still in your prayer life. If you don't move forward, you move backward. You either pray your way to a deeper relationship with God or you lose heart and ultimately give up on faith. True prayer never occurs apart from our sense of need. The very act of praying signals our dependence on God for our need. The purpose of prayer is to bring us to an understanding of the Father's heart. Prayer does not always lead us to an answer that satisfies our wants, desires, and curiosities. Prayer does, however, lead us to a place where we can accept that such answers are unnecessary to involving ourselves in the vast and mysterious purposes of the Father.

GET ON YOUR KNEES AND PRAY
by Kevin E. Heenan

When you're overloaded and down,
When things just don't go your way.
When darkness is all around,
Just get on your knees and pray.

If the world lets you down time and again,
And you never know the right words to say.
Don't you ever give up or give in,
Just get on your knees and pray.

If you're left lonely by this cruel world,
And it's a struggle to make it through the day.
The remedy available is simple,
It's to get on your knees and pray.

It doesn't matter wherever you are,
And it not the eloquence of what you say.
Bring to the Lord your thoughts and your heart,
As you get on your knees and pray.

The Lord wants you to give Him your all,
He wants all areas of your life, no matter how gray.
Take advantage of the opportunities God offers,
And get on your knees and pray.

The saint who advances on his knees never retreats,
And with God there is never a price to pay.
Come with a repentant and expectant heart,
As you get on your knees and pray.

STANDING ON THE
PROMISES OF GOD

T here was a wonderful song that was part of our worship service in church. The title was "Standing on the Promises of
Christ my King." It was written by a gentlemen named Russell
Kelso Carter in 1866 and has been published in 377 hymnals
across the world.

Here a few lines from the song:

> *Standing on the promises I cannot fall,*
> *Listening every moment to the Spirit's call,*
> *Resting in my Savior as my all in all,*
> *Standing on the promises of God.*
>
> *Standing, standing,*
> *Standing on the promises of God my Savior;*
> *Standing, standing,*
> *I'm standing on the promises of God.*

I decided to look into Scripture and find a few of the promises
that God makes to us through His Word, thirty-six of them
to be exact. There are countless others, but these are some of
my favorites. I've found that these promises are good to read

through and look over throughout my day for inspiration and keeping and trusting my faith in God to help me along.

"He gives strength to the weary and increases the power of the weak" (Isa. 40:29).

"'Though the mountains be shaken and the hills be removed, yet my unfailing love for you will not be shaken nor my covenant of peace be removed,' says the LORD, who has compassion on you" (Isa. 54:10).

"Submit yourselves, then, to God. Resist the devil, and he will flee from you" (James 4:7).

"If we confess our sins, He is faithful and just and will forgive us our sins and purify us from all unrighteousness" (1 John 1:9).

"If my people, who are called by my name, will humble them-selves and pray and seek My face and turn from their wicked ways, then I will hear from heaven, and I will forgive their sin and will heal their land" (2 Chron. 7:14).

"The LORD Himself goes before you and will be with you; He will never leave you nor forsake you. Do not be afraid; do not be discouraged" (Deut. 31:8).

"'For I know the plans I have for you,' declares the LORD, 'plans to prosper you and not to harm you, plans to give you hope and a future. Then you will call upon Me and come and pray to Me, and I will listen to you. You will seek Me and find Me when you seek Me with all your heart'" (Jer. 29:11–13).

"Whoever believes in the Son has eternal life, but whoever rejects the Son will not see life, for God's wrath remains on them" (John 3:36).

"'Bring the whole tithe into the storehouse, that there may be food in My house. Test me in this,' says the LORD Almighty, 'and see if I will not throw open the floodgates of heaven and pour out so much blessing that there will not be room enough to store it'" (Mal. 3:10).

"Therefore I tell you, whatever you ask for in prayer, believe that you have received it, and it will be yours" (Mark 11:24).

"Have I not commanded you? Be strong and courageous. Do not be afraid; do not be discouraged, for the LORD your God will be with you wherever you go" (Josh. 1:9).

"And my God will meet all your needs according to the riches of His glory in Christ Jesus" (Phil. 4:19).

"Even though I walk through the darkest valley, I will fear no evil, for You are with me; Your rod and Your staff, they comfort me" (Ps. 23:4).

"The LORD is my light and my salvation—whom shall I fear? The LORD is the stronghold of my life—of whom shall I be afraid?" (Ps. 27:1).

"The righteous cry out, and the LORD hears them; He delivers them from all their troubles" (Ps. 34:17).

"Take delight in the LORD, and He will give you the desires of your heart" (Ps. 37:4).

"You, Lord, are forgiving and good, abounding in love to all who call to You" (Ps. 86:5).

"And we know that in all things God works for the good of those who love Him, who have been called according to His purpose" (Rom. 8:28).

"If you declare with your mouth, 'Jesus is Lord,' and believe in your heart that God raised Him from the dead, you will be saved. For it is with your heart that you believe and are justified, and it is with your mouth that you profess your faith and are saved" (Rom. 10:9–10).

"The LORD is a refuge for the oppressed, a stronghold in times of trouble. Those who know Your name trust in You, for You, LORD, have never forsaken those who seek You" (Ps. 9:9–10).

"Do not be anxious about anything, but in every situation, by prayer and petition, with thanksgiving, present your requests to God. And the peace of God, which transcends all understanding, will guard your hearts and your minds in Christ Jesus" (Phil. 4:6–7).

"Trust in the LORD with all your heart and lean not on your own understanding; in all your ways submit to Him, and He will make your paths straight" (Prov. 3:5–6).

"But seek first His kingdom and His righteousness, and all these things will be given to you as well" (Matt. 6:33).

"Which of you, if your son asks for bread, will give him a stone? Or if he asks for a fish, will give him a snake? If you, then, though you are evil, know how to give good gifts to your children, how much more will your Father in heaven give good gifts to those who ask Him!" (Matt. 7:9–11).

"Praise the LORD, my soul, and forget not all His benefits—who forgives all your sins and heals all your diseases, who redeems your life from the pit and crowns you with love and compassion, who satisfies your desires with good things so that your youth is renewed like the eagle's" (Ps. 103:2–5).

"Then they cried to the LORD in their trouble, and He saved them from their distress. He brought them out of darkness, the utter darkness, and broke away their chains. Let them give thanks to the LORD for His unfailing love and His wonderful deeds for mankind, for He breaks down gates of bronze and cuts through bars of iron" (Ps. 107:13–16).

"And I will do whatever you ask in My name, so that the Father may be glorified in the Son. You may ask Me for anything in My name, and I will do it. If you love Me, keep My commands. And I will ask the Father, and He will give you another advocate to help you and be with you forever" (John 14:13–16).

"Come to Me, all you who are weary and burdened, and I will give you rest. Take My yoke upon you and learn from Me, for I

am gentle and humble in heart, and you will find rest for your souls" (Matt. 11:28–29).

"The LORD will fight for you; you need only to be still" (Ex. 14:14).

"So do not fear, for I am with you; do not be dismayed, for I am your God. I will strengthen you and help you; I will uphold you with My righteous right hand" (Isa. 41:10).

"For I am the LORD your God who takes hold of your right hand and says to you, 'Do not fear; I will help you'" (Isa. 41:13).

"When you pass through the waters, I will be with you; and when you pass through the rivers, they will not sweep over you. When you walk through the fire, you will not be burned; the flames will not set you ablaze" (Isa. 43:2).

"If any of you lacks wisdom, you should ask God, who gives generously to all without finding fault, and it will be given to you" (James 1:5).

Print these out on a separate piece of paper and carry these verses around for a while. More importantly, take them out and read them when you can. They'll be sure to lift your heart and hope as you trust on God's given promises.

PLAYERS AND COACHES ROSTER

Listed below are the names of the players and coaches I've met over this past decade. May God always bless these men in their future. My prayer is that you know that God wants you always to seek Him and to lean on Him. Thanks to all of you who have had an impact on my life.

Players:

Myles Smith #1
Noel Larkins #2
Chris Gorman #3
Preston Wynne #4
Selle Hann #5
Ennis Whatley Jr.#10
Brendan Holmes #12
Sean McCarthy #20
Taylor Kelly #23
Swing Chuang #24
Kirk Sheplay #30
Jordan Diandy #32
Tino Zaragoza #33
Preston Butler #42
Dakotah Richter #50
Logan Fougnies #20
Deangelo Jones #22
Zachary Kirschbaum RS*

Will Shannon #21
Kaleb Wilborn #50, #34
Sam Saufferer #1
Donte Williams #4
Connor Griffin #5
Capri Uzan #12
Mario Soto #23
Tiago Zibecchi #24
Jadan Anderson #30
Geremy McKay #40
James Moore #24
Ronald McQuay RS*
Absalom Barnes #0
Jonah Tolmaire #1
Dominic St. Leon #3
Aaron Byrne #5
Phillip Willis #4
Isaiah Gentry #12

Nuno Muandumba #10   Devon Riley #20
TJ Burke #12   Christian Wilson #32
Zach Allmon #23   Kieran Hayward #2
Keith Mason #42   Masie Mohammadi #3
Brandon Wiehe RS*   Aziz Seck #5
Malachi Hoosein #2   Michael Magee #10
John Staats #4   Jordan Hurst #20
Kwinn Hanson #40   Max Lawrence #23
Christian Ware-Berry #30   Nico Dasca #30
Nick Dalafu #20   Jon Scherer #22
Troy Deluca RS*   Juwan Ganiyu #34
Brandon Hood #3   Isaac Davis #1
Victor Evans #4   Luke Allen #2
Jaamon Echols #5   Isaiah Attles #10
Brandon Brothers #22   Timothy Bahadoor #12
Antonio Bishop #32   Jacob Brown #20
Connor Kennedy #33   Garrett White #33
Aubrey Myers Jr. #42   Jadyn Johnson #40
Connor Metcalfe #44   Andre Allen #2
Billy Keller#1   Jordan Caruso #5
Teslim Idris #5   Isaac Padilla #10
Shacquille Dawkins #10   Kody Knox #23
Jamaal Lee #32   Alex Davis #42
Will Ball #40   RS* Red Shirt

Coaches:

Rhett Soliday, Head Coach, 2010-present
Kevin Heenan, Assistant Coach, 2012-present
Brian Boomer Roberts, Assistant Coach, 2010-2014
Levi Seekins, Assistant Coach, 2010-2013
George Tuttle, Assistant Coach, 2011-2019
Brad Davis, Assistant Coach, 2013-2018
Shacolby Randell, Assistant Coach, 2013-2015
Richard Solte, Assistant Coach,2013-2015

Taylor Kelly, Assistant Coach, 2014-2020
Kirk Sheplay, Assistant Coach2014-2016
Selle Hann, Assistant Coach, 2018-2020
Shawn Harris, Assistant Coach, 2016-2018
James Larson, Assistant Coach, 2016-2018
Andre Klun, Assistant Coach, 2016-2018
Connor Metcalfe, Assistant Coach, 2016-2017
Kwinn Hanson, Assistant Coach, 2017-2018
Brian Kim, Assistant Coach, 2017-2018
Justin Downer, Assistant Coach, 2018-2019
Lyle McIntosh, Assistant Coach, 2018-2020
Colton Kooima, Assistant Coach, 2019-2021
Connor Vandyken, Assistant Coach, 2019-2020
Manny Gallegos, Assistant Coach, 2019-2021
Noel Larkins, Assistant Coach, 2020-present
Andre Murillo, Assistant Coach, 2020-present
Jordan Wild, Assistant Coach, 2021-present
Billy Thompson, Assistant Coach, 2021 to present
Connor Tuttle, Assistant Coach, 2021 to present
Rand Rowland, Assistant Coach, 2021 to present

LEAN ON ME
By Kevin E. Heenan

Lean on Me when you're not feeling strong,
As you go through your life, please take Me along.
Let Me be with you during the course of your day,
Allow Me in to your heart and listen to what I say.

Let your soul become one with Me,
For My love for you is forever, let Me in, let Me be.
You will see just how much I care,
When you feel Me taking on burdens you simply can't bear.

I'll lift you high and above those doubting ways,
Just come to Me each and every day.
When you lift up your thoughts from down on your knees,
I will give you that comfort that comes only from Me.

Your days will be special and filled with delight,
I'll look over your life and make it all right.
I am there when you need Me, trust Me and see,
Your life will be blessed when you lean on Me.

CPSIA information can be obtained
at www.ICGtesting.com
Printed in the USA
BVHW061745300422
635802BV00005B/101